The How-To Handbook for Jewish Living

Rabbi Kerry M. Olitzky
and
Rabbi Ronald H. Isaacs

Illustrations by
Dorcas Gelabert

KTAV Publishing House, Inc.
Hoboken, New Jersey

Copyright © 1993
Kerry M. Olitzky & Ronald H. Isaacs
Library of Congress Cataloging-in-Publication Data

Olitzky, Kerry M.
  The how to handbook for Jewish living / by Kerry M. Olitzky and
Ronald H. Isaacs.
    p. cm.
  ISBN 0-88125-290-5 (pbk.) : $12.95.--ISBN 0-88125-294-8 : $24.95
  1. Judaism--Customs and practices. 2. Jewish way of life.
I. Isaacs, Ronald H. II. Title.
BM700.O43 1993
296.7'4--dc20
                                       93-14594
                                         CIP

Manufactured in the United States of America
KTAV Publishing House, Inc., 900 Jefferson St., Hoboken, NJ 07030

Table of Contents

Preface

We learn best by example, observing the way things are done by our families, friends, and neighbors. When that is not possible, we turn to books in order to guide us and even reinforce our learning. But where do you go to find out all of the basic things you need to know to live the life of a Jew? There is really no one place—until now! In the pages of this book, you will find a step-by-step guide to doing things that make us unique as Jewish people. Just about all you need to know is included. And if you are so inclined, we have included basic sources and books to read if you want to know more. When the sources for a particular practice come to us through various paths in Jewish history and culture, we have listed only those that we feel are most relevant to you (and your teacher or parent). We have also included a section called "Instant Information" for those hard-to-find pieces of information that you just have to know but have no idea where to turn for the answer.

If you are just returning to Judaism and find all of these practices overwhelming, start with one today and two tomorrow. Judaism is a rich experience. We just want to get you started. This book is here to help.

Rabbi Ronald H. Isaacs
Rabbi Kerry M. Olitzky

Basic Berachot (Blessings)
בְּרָכוֹת

The source:

Berachot (Blessings) are attributed to the Men of the Great
Assembly, who lived approximately 400–300 B.C.E.

What you need to know:

According to the great medieval Jewish philosopher
Moses Maimonides (known as the RaMBaM), there are
three types of blessings:

1. Blessings recited prior to eating, drinking, or smelling   בְּרְכוֹת הַנֶּהֱנִין
   nice things, called *Birchot Hanehenin.*

2. Blessings recited prior to the performance of a mitz-   בְּרְכוֹת הַמִּצְווֹת
   vah, known as *Birchot Hamitzvot.*

3. Blessings that express praise of God and thanks to   בְּרְכוֹת הוֹדָאָה
   God, as well as those that ask God for things, called
   Birchot Hodaah.

בְּרְכוֹת הַנֶּהֱנִין
Birchot Hanehenin

Blessings for Taste

On eating bread:

בָּרוּךְ אַתָּה יְיָ אֱלֹהֵינוּ מֶלֶךְ הָעוֹלָם, הַמּוֹצִיא לֶחֶם מִן הָאָרֶץ.

*Baruch atah Adonai elohaynu melech ha'olam hamotzi
lechem min ha'aretz.*

Praised are You, Adonai our God, Sovereign of the
Universe, who brings forth bread from the earth.

1

On eating foods other than bread prepared from wheat, barley, rye, oats, or spelt (such as cakes and cookies):

בָּרוּךְ אַתָּה יְיָ אֱלֹהֵינוּ מֶלֶךְ הָעוֹלָם, בּוֹרֵא מִינֵי מְזוֹנוֹת.

Baruch atah Adonai elohaynu melech ha'olam boray meenay mezonote.

Praised are You, Adonai our God, Sovereign of the Universe, who creates different kinds of nourishment.

On drinking wine:

בָּרוּךְ אַתָּה יְיָ אֱלֹהֵינוּ מֶלֶךְ הָעוֹלָם, בּוֹרֵא פְּרִי הַגָּפֶן.

Baruch atah Adonai elohaynu melech ha'olam boray pri ha'gafen.

Praised are You, Adonai our God, Sovereign of the Universe, who creates the fruit of the vine.

On eating fruit:

בָּרוּךְ אַתָּה יְיָ אֱלֹהֵינוּ מֶלֶךְ הָעוֹלָם, בּוֹרֵא פְּרִי הָעֵץ.

Baruch atah Adonai elohaynu melech ha'olam boray pri ha'eytz.

Praised are You, Adonai our God, Sovereign of the Universe, who creates the fruit of the tree.

On eating foods which grow in the ground, like potatoes:

בָּרוּךְ אַתָּה יְיָ אֱלֹהֵינוּ מֶלֶךְ הָעוֹלָם, בּוֹרֵא פְּרִי הָאֲדָמָה.

Baruch atah Adonai elohaynu melech ha'olam boray pri ha'adamah.

Praised are You, Adonai our God, Sovereign of the Universe, who creates the fruit of the ground.

A general blessing for other food and drink:

בָּרוּךְ אַתָּה יְיָ אֱלֹהֵינוּ מֶלֶךְ הָעוֹלָם, שֶׁהַכֹּל נִהְיָה בִּדְבָרוֹ.

Baruch atah Adonai elohaynu melech ha'olam she'hakol nihiyeh bidvaro.

Praised are you, Adonai our God, Sovereign of the Universe, at whose word all things come into existence.

Blessings for Smell

On smelling fragrant spices:

בָּרוּךְ אַתָּה יְיָ אֱלֹהֵינוּ מֶלֶךְ הָעוֹלָם, בּוֹרֵא מִינֵי בְשָׂמִים.

Baruch atah Adonai elohaynu melech ha'olam boray minay vesamim.

Praised are You, Adonai our God, Sovereign of the Universe, who creates different kinds of spices.

On smelling the fragrance of shrubs and trees:

בָּרוּךְ אַתָּה יְיָ אֱלֹהֵינוּ מֶלֶךְ הָעוֹלָם, בּוֹרֵא עֲצֵי בְשָׂמִים.

Baruch atah Adonai elohaynu melech ha'olam boray atzay vesamim.

Praised are You, Adonai our God, Sovereign of the Universe, who creates fragrant trees.

On smelling the fragrances of plants and herbs:

בָּרוּךְ אַתָּה יְיָ אֱלֹהֵינוּ מֶלֶךְ הָעוֹלָם, בּוֹרֵא עִשְׂבֵי בְשָׂמִים.

Baruch atah Adonai elohaynu melech ha'olam boray isvay vesamim.

Praised are You, Adonai our God, Sovereign of the Universe, who creates fragrant plants.

On smelling fragrant fruit:

בָּרוּךְ אַתָּה יְיָ אֱלֹהֵינוּ מֶלֶךְ הָעוֹלָם, הַנּוֹתֵן רֵיחַ טוֹב בַּפֵּרוֹת.

Baruch atah Adonai elohaynu melech ha'olam hanotayn rayach tov bapayrot.

Praised are You, Adonai our God, Sovereign of the Universe, who gives a pleasant fragrance to fruits.

On smelling fragrant oils:

בָּרוּךְ אַתָּה יְיָ אֱלֹהֵינוּ מֶלֶךְ הָעוֹלָם, בּוֹרֵא שֶׁמֶן עָרֵב.

Baruch atah Adonai elohaynu melech ha'olam boray she-men arayv.

Praised are You, Adonai our God, Sovereign of the Universe, who creates fragrant oil.

Blessings for Seeing Special Things

On seeing a rainbow:

בָּרוּךְ אַתָּה יְיָ אֱלֹהֵינוּ מֶלֶךְ הָעוֹלָם, זוֹכֵר הַבְּרִית וְנֶאֱמָן בִּבְרִיתוֹ וְקַיָּם בְּמַאֲמָרוֹ.

Baruch atah Adonai elohaynu melech ha'olam zocher ha'berit ve'ne'eman bivrito vekayam be'ma'amaro.

Praised are You, Adonai our God, Sovereign of the Universe, who remembers the covenant and is faithful in keeping promises.

On seeing trees blossoming for the first time in the year:

בָּרוּךְ אַתָּה יְיָ אֱלֹהֵינוּ מֶלֶךְ הָעוֹלָם, שֶׁלֹּא חִסַּר בְּעוֹלָמוֹ דָּבָר, וּבָרָא בוֹ בְּרִיּוֹת טוֹבוֹת וְאִילָנוֹת טוֹבִים לְהַנּוֹת בָּהֶם בְּנֵי אָדָם.

Baruch atah Adonai elohaynu melech ha'olam shelo chisar b'olamo davar uvara vo briyot tovot v'ilanot tovim l'hanot bahem b'nai adam.

Praised are You, Adonai our God, Sovereign of the Universe, who has withheld nothing from the world, and has created lovely creatures and beautiful trees for people to enjoy.

4

On seeing the ocean:

בָּרוּךְ אַתָּה יְיָ אֱלֹהֵינוּ מֶלֶךְ הָעוֹלָם, שֶׁעָשָׂה אֶת־הַיָּם הַגָּדוֹל.

Baruch atah Adonai elohaynu melech ha'olam she-asah et hayam hagadol.

Praised are You, Adonai our God, Sovereign of the Universe, who has made the great sea.

On seeing trees or creatures of unusual beauty:

בָּרוּךְ אַתָּה יְיָ אֱלֹהֵינוּ מֶלֶךְ הָעוֹלָם, שֶׁכֵּכָה לוֹ בְּעוֹלָמוֹ.

Baruch atah Adonai elohaynu melech ha'olam shekacha lo b'olamo.

Praised are You, Adonai our God, Sovereign of the Universe, who has such beauty in the world.

On seeing someone of abnormal appearance:

בָּרוּךְ אַתָּה יְיָ אֱלֹהֵינוּ מֶלֶךְ הָעוֹלָם, מְשַׁנֶּה הַבְּרִיוֹת.

Baruch atah Adonai elohaynu melech ha'olam mishaneh ha'briyot.

Praised are You, Adonai our God, Sovereign of the Universe, who makes people different.

On seeing lightning, shooting stars, mountains, or sunrises:

בָּרוּךְ אַתָּה יְיָ אֱלֹהֵינוּ מֶלֶךְ הָעוֹלָם, עֹשֶׂה מַעֲשֵׂה בְרֵאשִׁית.

Baruch atah Adonai elahaynu melech ha'olam oseh ma'asey v'reshit.

Praised are You, Adonai our God, Sovereign of the Universe, Source of creation.

On seeing restored synagogues:

בָּרוּךְ אַתָּה יְיָ אֱלֹהֵינוּ מֶלֶךְ הָעוֹלָם, מַצִּיב גְּבוּל אַלְמָנָה.

Baruch atah Adonai elohaynu melech ha'olam matziv gevul almanah.

Praised are You, Adonai our God, Sovereign of the Universe, who restores the borders of the widow [Zion].

On seeing a person who is really knowledgeable about Torah:

בָּרוּךְ אַתָּה יְיָ אֱלֹהֵינוּ מֶלֶךְ הָעוֹלָם, שֶׁחָלַק מֵחָכְמָתוֹ לִירֵאָיו.

Baruch atah Adonai elohaynu melech ha'olam shechalak me'chochmato lirey'av.

Praised are You, Adonai our God, Sovereign of the Universe, who has given wisdom to those who revere God.

On seeing a person who knows lots of things about lots of things:

בָּרוּךְ אַתָּה יְיָ אֱלֹהֵינוּ מֶלֶךְ הָעוֹלָם, שֶׁנָּתַן מֵחָכְמָתוֹ לְבָשָׂר וָדָם.

Baruch atah Adonai elohaynu melech ha'olam she'natan me-chochmato l'vasar va'dam.

Praised are You, Adonai our God, Sovereign of the Universe, who has given wisdom to human beings.

On seeing a head of state (like a president):

בָּרוּךְ אַתָּה יְיָ אֱלֹהֵינוּ מֶלֶךְ הָעוֹלָם, שֶׁנָּתַן מִכְּבוֹדוֹ לְבָשָׂר וָדָם.

Baruch atah Adonai elohaynu melech ha'olam she'natan mi'kvodo l'vasar va'dam.

Praised are You, Adonai our God, Sovereign of the Universe, who has given special status to human beings.

6

Blessings on Hearing Something Special

On hearing thunder:

בָּרוּךְ אַתָּה יְיָ אֱלֹהֵינוּ מֶלֶךְ הָעוֹלָם, שֶׁכֹּחוֹ וּגְבוּרָתוֹ מָלֵא עוֹלָם.

Baruch atah Adonai elohaynu melech ha'olam she'kocho u'gevurato malay olam.

Praised are You, Adonai our God, Sovereign of the Universe, whose mighty power fills the entire world.

On hearing good news:

בָּרוּךְ אַתָּה יְיָ אֱלֹהֵינוּ מֶלֶךְ הָעוֹלָם, הַטּוֹב וְהַמֵּטִיב.

Baruch atah Adonai elohaynu melech ha'olam hatov v'hametiv.

Praised are You, Adonai our God, Sovereign of the Universe, who is good and causes good things to happen.

On hearing tragic news:

בָּרוּךְ אַתָּה יְיָ אֱלֹהֵינוּ מֶלֶךְ הָעוֹלָם, דַּיַּן הָאֱמֶת.

Baruch atah Adonai elohaynu melech ha'olam dayan ha-emet.

Praised are You, Adonai our God, Sovereign of the Universe, who is the true Judge.

בִּרְכוֹת הַמִּצְוֹת
Birchot Hamitzvot

On lighting Shabbat candles:

בָּרוּךְ אַתָּה יְיָ אֱלֹהֵינוּ מֶלֶךְ הָעוֹלָם, אֲשֶׁר קִדְּשָׁנוּ בְּמִצְוֹתָיו, וְצִוָּנוּ לְהַדְלִיק נֵר שֶׁל שַׁבָּת.

Baruch atah Adonai elohaynu melech ha'olam asher kidshanu be'mitzvotav vetzivanu l'hadlik ner shel Shabbat.

7

Praised are You, Adonai our God, Sovereign of the Universe, who has made us holy with mitzvot and instructed us to light Sabbath candles.

On lighting holiday candles:

בָּרוּךְ אַתָּה יְיָ אֱלֹהֵינוּ מֶלֶךְ הָעוֹלָם, אֲשֶׁר קִדְּשָׁנוּ בְּמִצְוֹתָיו, וְצִוָּנוּ לְהַדְלִיק נֵר שֶׁל יוֹם טוֹב.

Baruch atah Adonai elohaynu melech ha'olam asher kidshanu be'mitzvotav vetzivanu l'hadlik ner shel yom tov.

Praised are You, Adonai our God, Sovereign of the Universe, who has made us holy with mitzvot and instructed us to light festival candles.

On washing hands:

בָּרוּךְ אַתָּה יְיָ אֱלֹהֵינוּ מֶלֶךְ הָעוֹלָם, אֲשֶׁר קִדְּשָׁנוּ בְּמִצְוֹתָיו, וְצִוָּנוּ עַל נְטִילַת יָדָיִם.

Baruch atah Adonai elohaynu melech ha'olam asher kidshanu bemitzvotav vetzivanu al netilat yadayim.

Praised are You, Adonai our God, Sovereign of the Universe, who has made us holy with mitzvot and instructed us to wash our hands.

בִּרְכוֹת הוֹדָאָה
Birchot Hodaah

1. בָּרוּךְ אַתָּה יְיָ אֱלֹהֵינוּ מֶלֶךְ הָעוֹלָם, אֲשֶׁר נָתַן לַשֶּׂכְוִי בִינָה לְהַבְחִין בֵּין יוֹם וּבֵין לָיְלָה.
2. בָּרוּךְ אַתָּה יְיָ אֱלֹהֵינוּ מֶלֶךְ הָעוֹלָם, שֶׁעָשַׂנִי בְּצַלְמוֹ.
3. בָּרוּךְ אַתָּה יְיָ אֱלֹהֵינוּ מֶלֶךְ הָעוֹלָם, שֶׁעָשַׂנִי יִשְׂרָאֵל.
4. בָּרוּךְ אַתָּה יְיָ אֱלֹהֵינוּ מֶלֶךְ הָעוֹלָם, שֶׁעָשַׂנִי בֶּן־ (בַּת־)חוֹרִין.
5. בָּרוּךְ אַתָּה יְיָ אֱלֹהֵינוּ מֶלֶךְ הָעוֹלָם, פּוֹקֵחַ עִוְרִים.
6. בָּרוּךְ אַתָּה יְיָ אֱלֹהֵינוּ מֶלֶךְ הָעוֹלָם, מַלְבִּישׁ עֲרֻמִּים.
7. בָּרוּךְ אַתָּה יְיָ אֱלֹהֵינוּ מֶלֶךְ הָעוֹלָם, מַתִּיר אֲסוּרִים.
8. בָּרוּךְ אַתָּה יְיָ אֱלֹהֵינוּ מֶלֶךְ הָעוֹלָם, זוֹקֵף כְּפוּפִים.

9. בָּרוּךְ אַתָּה יְיָ אֱלֹהֵינוּ מֶלֶךְ הָעוֹלָם, רוֹקַע הָאָרֶץ עַל הַמָּיִם.

10. בָּרוּךְ אַתָּה יְיָ אֱלֹהֵינוּ מֶלֶךְ הָעוֹלָם, שֶׁעָשָׂה לִי כָּל־צָרְכִּי.

11. בָּרוּךְ אַתָּה יְיָ אֱלֹהֵינוּ מֶלֶךְ הָעוֹלָם, הַמֵּכִין מִצְעֲדֵי־גָבֶר.

12. בָּרוּךְ אַתָּה יְיָ אלֹהֵינוּ מֶלֶךְ הָעוֹלָם, אוֹזֵר יִשְׂרָאֵל בִּגְבוּרָה.

13. בָּרוּךְ אַתָּה יְיָ אֱלֹהֵינוּ מֶלֶךְ הָעוֹלָם, עוֹטֵר יִשְׂרָאֵל בְּתִפְאָרָה.

14. בָּרוּךְ אַתָּה יְיָ אֱלֹהֵינוּ מֶלֶךְ הָעוֹלָם, הַנּוֹתֵן לַיָּעֵף כֹּחַ.

Praised are You, Adonai our God, Sovereign of the Universe:

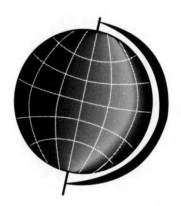

1. . . . who helps Your creatures distinguish day and night.
2. . . . who made me in God's image.
3. . . . who made me a Jew.
4. . . . who made me a free person.
5. . . . who gives sight to blind people.
6. . . . who clothes the naked.
7. . . . who releases the imprisoned.
8. . . . who raises the downtrodden.
9. . . . who creates heaven and earth.
10. . . . who provides me with everything.
11. . . . who guides us on our path.
12. . . . who strengthens Israel with courage.
13. . . . who gives Israel glory.
14. . . . who restores strength to those who are tired.

Things to remember:

1. Blessings can be said in any language as long as they express thoughts similar to the Hebrew text and include the basic formula "Praised are You, Adonai our God, who. . . בָּרוּךְ אַתָּה יְיָ אֱלֹהֵינוּ מֶלֶךְ הָעוֹלָם."

2. In blessings related to eating, smelling, or the performance of a mitzvah, the blessing is recited first followed by the specific action. However, in the case of Sabbath candles, light them first and then say the blessing (with your eyes covered).

Key words and phrases:

Beracha בְּרָכָה. Blessing (plural, *berachot* בְּרָכוֹת)
Birchot hamitzvot בִּרְכוֹת הַמִּצְוֹת. Blessings said prior to the performance of a mitzvah.

Birchot hanehenin בִּרְכוֹת הַנֶּהֱנִין. Blessings said prior to eating, drinking, smelling, and so forth.

Birchot hashachar בִּרְכוֹת הַשַּׁחַר. Blessings of the morning (literally, "at dawn").

Birchot hodaah בִּרְכוֹת הוֹדָאָה. Blessings that speak of praise of God and thanks to God, or that ask God for specific things.

If you want to know more:

Steven M. Brown, *Higher and Higher* (New York, 1979).

Hayim Donin, *To Pray as a Jew* (New York, 1980).

Joel Grishaver, *Basic Berachot* (Los Angeles, 1988).

Isaac Klein, *A Guide to Jewish Religious Practice* (New York, 1979).

Richard Siegel, Michael Strassfeld, and Sharon Strassfeld, *The First Jewish Catalogue* (Philadelphia, 1973).

The Rubrics of Prayer
תְּפִילָה

The source:

"As for me, let my prayer be for You, God, in an acceptable time" (Ps. 69:14).

The beginnings of the order of prayer are found in the second part of the talmudic tractate *Berachot,* which is a compilation from the period of the first *geonim.*

What you need to know:

OUTLINE OF DAILY MORNING SERVICE

Early Morning Blessings בִּרְכוֹת הַשַּׁחַר

Hymns and psalms to prepare us for prayer	*Baruch She'amar* בָּרוּךְ שֶׁאָמַר Selected Psalms תְּהִלִּים *Yishtabach* יִשְׁתַּבַּח
	Barechu בָּרְכוּ (Call to Prayer)
שְׁמַע יִשְׂרָאֵל *Shema Yisrael* and its blessings	First blessing before *Shema* שְׁמַע—*Yotzer Or* יוֹצֵר אוֹר (God creates light every day anew)
	Second blessing before *Shema* שְׁמַע— *Ahava Rabba* אַהֲבָה רַבָּה (God gives us the Torah and shows us love)

Shema שְׁמַע

	Deut. 6:4–9
Three paragraphs	Deut. 11:13–21
	Num. 15:37–41

Blessing after *Shema* שְׁמַע–*Ga'al Yisrael* גָּאַל יִשְׂרָאֵל (God redeems Israel)

Amida עֲמִידָה, also known as the *Shemoneh Esray* שְׁמוֹנֶה עֶשְׂרֵה or *Hatefillah* הַתְּפִילָה

Torah reading קְרִיאַת הַתּוֹרָה (Monday and Thursday)

Full *Kaddish* קַדִּישׁ שָׁלֵם

Aleynu עָלֵינוּ

Mourner's *Kaddish* קַדִּישׁ יָתוֹם

Prayer Choreography

When (i.e, during which prayer)	What to do	How to do it	Why
In general	Shuckling	Swaying back and forth on your feet	To involve all of your heart and soul in prayer
Barechu	Bowing	Bow from the waist on the word *barechu*	Like bowing before a sovereign
Shema Yisrael Adonai Elohaynu Adonai Echad	Closing your eyes	Cover your eyes with your right hand	To keep away from distraction and concentrate on God's Oneness
Third paragraph of the *Shema* (i.e., *Vayomer Adonai*)	Kissing *tzitzit* (fringes)	Gather *tzitzit* and kiss them at each mention of *tzitzit* in third paragraph of *Shema*	To symbolically embrace God's *mitzvot*
Adonai sifatai tiftach ufi yagid tihilatecha (verse before the *Amida*)	Approaching God	Walk back three steps and then forward three steps	To symbolically approach the Sovereign
Baruch atah Adonai elohaynu vaylohay avotaynu (beginning of *Amida*)	Bowing	Bend knees at *baruch,* bend over your waist at *atah,* and straighten up at *Adonai* (see fig. 1)	To bow before God the Sovereign

Baruch atah Adonai magen Avraham (second blessing in *Amida*)	Bowing	Same as above	Same as above
Kedusha on words *Kadosh, kadosh, kadosh*	Rise on tip-toes at each mention of the word *kadosh*		To symbolically reach toward heaven
Modim anachnu lach (in *Amida*)	Bowing	Same as first blessing of *Amida*	Same as for bowing
Baruch atah Adonai hatov shimcha ulecha na'eh lehodot (in *Amida*)	Bowing	Same as above	Same as above
Oseh shalom bimromav hu yaaseh shalom alenu ve'al kol Yisrael veimru amen	Taking leave of God	Take three steps backward: at *shalom bimromav* bend your head and shoulders to the left; at *hu yaaseh shalom* bend your head and shoulders to the right; at *alenu ve'al kol Yisrael* bend your head and shoulders forward; at *veimru* stand erect.	This is the reverse of the approach to God at beginning of *Amida*. Here we take leave of God.
Alenu, on words *va'anachnu korim umishtachavim umodim*	Bow	Bend knees at *va'anachnu korim*; bow at *umishtachavim*, stand erect at *lifnay melech* (see fig. below)	We show humility to God, the Sovereign of all Sovereigns

Key words and phrases:

Birchot hashachar בִּרְכוֹת הַשַׁחַר. Blessings of the morning.

Matbe'ah shel tefillah מַטְבֵּעַ שֶׁל תְּפִילָה. Sacred order of the prayer service.

Pesukai d'zimra פְּסוּקֵי דְזִמְרָה. Prayers in the Preliminary Service.

Tehillim תְּהִלִּים. Psalms.

If you want to know more:

Philip Arian and Azriel Eisenberg, *The Story of the Prayer Book* (Bridgeport, Conn., 1968).

Steven Brown, *Higher and Higher: Making Jewish Prayer Part of Us* (New York, 1979).

Hayim Donin, *To Pray as a Jew* (New York, 1980).

Harvey Fields, *Bechol Levavcha: With All Your Heart* (New York, 1976).

Isaac Klein, *A Guide to Jewish Religious Practice* (New York, 1979).

More particulars:

1. Correct way to bow for *Baruch atah Adonai* בָּרוּךְ אַתָּה ה'. When one bends the knees it is at *baruch* בָּרוּךְ (blessed); and when one straightens up it is at God's name (*Shulchan Aruch, Orach Chayim* 113:7).

Baruch   Ata   Adonai

2. Correct way to bow for *Aleynu* עָלֵינוּ

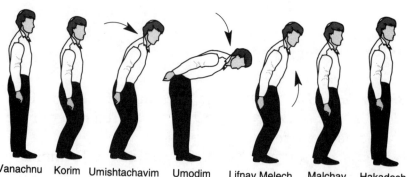

Vanachnu   Korim   Umishtachavim   Umodim   Lifnay Melech   Malchay Hamlachim   Hakadosh Baruch hu

How to Make Aliyah to the Torah
עֲלִיָּה לַתּוֹרָה

The source:

Code of Jewish Law (*Shulchan Aruch, Orach Chayim* 139–141); Babylonian Talmud, Megillah 31b–32a.

What you need to know:

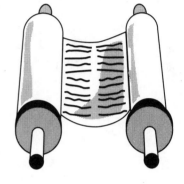

1. After your name has been called, go up to the Torah, to the left side of the reader. After the *baal koreh* (Torah reader) has shown you the place about to be read, touch it with the *tzitzit* (fringes) of your *tallit* (or with the spine of your *siddur*). The scroll will next be rolled together. Stand behind the Torah scroll and say the following blessing:

בָּרְכוּ אֶת יְיָ הַמְּבֹרָךְ:

Barechu et Adonai hamevorach.

Praise Adonai, to whom our praise is due!

בָּרוּךְ יְיָ הַמְּבֹרָךְ לְעוֹלָם וָעֶד:

Baruch Adonai ha'mevorach le-olam va'ed.

Praised be Adonai, to whom our praise is due, now and forever!

בָּרוּךְ אַתָּה יְיָ אֱלֹהֵינוּ מֶלֶךְ הָעוֹלָם אֲשֶׁר בָּחַר בָּנוּ מִכָּל הָעַמִּים וְנָתַן לָנוּ אֶת תּוֹרָתוֹ: בָּרוּךְ אַתָּה יְיָ נוֹתֵן הַתּוֹרָה:

Baruch atah Adonai elohaynu melech ha'olam asher bachar banu mikol ha'amim ve'natan lanu et torahto Baruch atah Adonai notayn ha-Torah.

Praised is Adonai our God, Sovereign of the Universe, who has chosen us from all peoples by giving us Torah. Praised is Adonai, Giver of the Torah.

Then move to the right of the *baal koreh* so the Torah can be read.

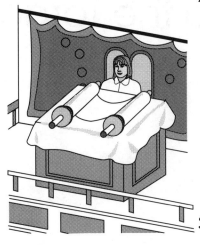

2. After the reading, recite the following:

בָּרוּךְ אַתָּה יְיָ אֱלֹהֵינוּ מֶלֶךְ הָעוֹלָם אֲשֶׁר נָתַן לָנוּ תּוֹרַת אֱמֶת וְחַיֵּי עוֹלָם נָטַע בְּתוֹכֵנוּ: בָּרוּךְ אַתָּה יְיָ נוֹתֵן הַתּוֹרָה:

Baruch atah Adonai elohaynu melech ha'olam asher natan lanu torat emet ve'chayai olam nata bitochaynu. Baruch atah Adonai notayn ha-Torah.

Praised is Adonai our God, Sovereign of the Universe, who has given us a Torah of truth, implanting within us eternal life. Praised is Adonai, Giver of the Torah.

3. Then stay on the left side of the reader during the next *aliyah.*

יַשֵׁר כֹּחַ
בָּרוּךְ תִּהְיֶה

4. Following the next *aliyah,* you may go back to your seat. People will say to you *yasher koach* "May you be strengthened." You should respond *baruch tihyeh,* "May it be blessed."

Things to remember:

בֶּן
בַּת

1. In order to be called to the Torah, the rabbi will want to know your Hebrew name (___ son/daughter of ___ and ___).

2. In many synagogues, people are called in order of their priestly legacy (Cohen, Levi, and Israelite). In their quest for equality, Reform synagogues, Reconstructionist and some Conservative ones have generally discontinued this distinction.

בִּרְכַּת הַגּוֹמֵל
מִי שֶׁבֵּרַךְ

3. Following your *aliyah,* one says *Birkat Ha-gomel* if appropriate (see below, p. 45). Blessings for health, recovery and the like (*mi sheberach*) are said at this time also.

בִּימָה

4. Some people descend the *bimah* backwards so as not to turn their back on the Ark—like exiting from an audience with a king.

עֵץ חַיִּים
תּוֹרָתוֹ

5. Some people hold the *etz chaim* while reciting the blessing and actually raise the scroll slightly on the word *Torahto.*

6. Here is the music to help you remember how the
   blessings for an *aliyah* are to be sung.

First Blessing.

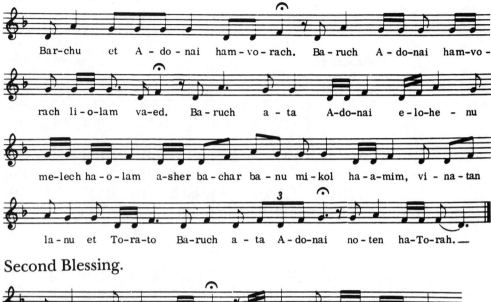

Bar-chu   et   A - do - nai   ham-vo - rach.   Ba - ruch   A - do - nai   ham-vo-
rach li - o - lam   va-ed.   Ba - ruch   a - ta   A - do - nai   e - lo - he - nu
me-lech ha - o - lam   a-sher ba - char ba - nu   mi-kol   ha - a-mim,   vi - na - tan
la - nu   et   To - ra - to   Ba - ruch   a - ta   A - do - nai   no - ten   ha - To - rah.

Second Blessing.

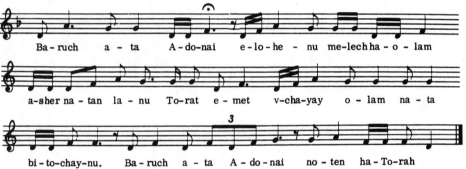

Ba - ruch   a - ta   A - do - nai   e - lo - he - nu   me-lech ha - o - lam
a-sher na - tan   la - nu   To - rat   e - met   v - cha - yay   o - lam   na - ta
bi - to - chay-nu.   Ba - ruch   a - ta   A - do - nai   no - ten   ha - To - rah

Key words and phrases:

Aliyah עֲלִיָה. Going up to the Torah, a Torah honor (also
    means emigrating to Israel).

Baal koreh בַּעַל קוֹרֵא. Torah reader.

Etz chaim עֵץ חַיִּים. Torah roller.

Gabbai גַבַּאי. The person in a synagogue who makes things
    run smoothly during the services by assigning *aliyot*
    (plural of *aliyah*) and corrects the mistakes of the
    person reading the Torah.

If you want to know more:

Encyclopaedia Judaica (Jerusalem, 1971) 15:1253–1254.

Hayim Donin, *To Pray as a Jew* (New York, 1980).

Rose Goldstein, *A Time to Pray* (Bridgeport, Conn., 1972).

Isaac Klein, *A Guide to Jewish Religious Practice* (New York,
    1979).

Putting on Tefillin
תְּפִלִּין

The sources:

וְהָיָה לְךָ לְאוֹת עַל־יָדְךָ וּלְזִכָּרוֹן בֵּין עֵינֶיךָ לְמַעַן תִּהְיֶה תּוֹרַת יְהֹוָה בְּפִיךָ כִּי בְּיָד חֲזָקָה הוֹצִאֲךָ יְהֹוָה מִמִּצְרָיִם:

"And it shall serve you as a sign on your hand and as a reminder on your forehead—in order that the teachings of Adonai may be in your mouth—that with a mighty hand Adonai freed you from Egypt" (Exod. 13:9).

וְהָיָה לְאוֹת עַל־יָדְכָה וּלְטוֹטָפֹת בֵּין עֵינֶיךָ כִּי בְּחֹזֶק יָד הוֹצִיאָנוּ יְהֹוָה מִמִּצְרָיִם:

"And so it shall be as a sign upon your hand and as a symbol on your forehead that with a mighty hand Adonai freed us from Egypt" (Exod. 13:16).

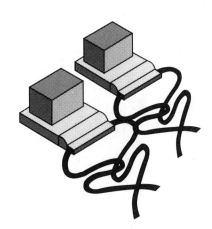

וּקְשַׁרְתָּם לְאוֹת עַל־יָדֶךָ וְהָיוּ לְטֹטָפֹת בֵּין עֵינֶיךָ: וּכְתַבְתָּם עַל־מְזֻזוֹת בֵּיתֶךָ וּבִשְׁעָרֶיךָ:

"Bind them as a sign on your hand and let them serve as a symbol on your forehead" (Deut. 6:8).

וְשַׂמְתֶּם אֶת־דְּבָרַי אֵלֶּה עַל־לְבַבְכֶם וְעַל־נַפְשְׁכֶם וּקְשַׁרְתֶּם אֹתָם לְאוֹת עַל־יֶדְכֶם וְהָיוּ לְטוֹטָפֹת בֵּין עֵינֵיכֶם:

"Therefore impress these My words upon your very heart: bind them as a sign on your hand and let them serve as a symbol on your forehead" (Deut. 11:18).

What you need to know:

1. To begin, roll up the sleeve (if you have one) of your weaker arm (the one you don't write with) to above your biceps muscle. Take off any jewelry (watches, rings) which you can put on your other hand.

2. Unwrap the straps of the hand *tefillin* (*tefillin shel yad*). Place the *tefillin* box (*bayit*) on the biceps of your upper arm, with the leather piece (*maabarta*) that sticks out on the side closest to your shoulder. The knot (*kesher*) should be placed on the top of your biceps muscle on the side closest to your body. When everything is in place, say this blessing:

תְּפִלִּין שֶׁל יָד
בַּיִת
מַעֲבַּרְתָּא
קֶשֶׁר

בָּרוּךְ אַתָּה יְיָ אֱלֹהֵינוּ מֶלֶךְ הָעוֹלָם אֲשֶׁר קִדְּשָׁנוּ בְּמִצְוֹתָיו וְצִוָּנוּ לְהָנִיחַ תְּפִלִּין:

Baruch atah Adonai elohaynu melech ha'olam asher kid-shanu bemitzvotav vetzivanu lehani'ach tefillin.

Praised are You, Adonai our God, Sovereign of the Universe, who has made us holy with mitzvot and instructed us to wear *tefillin.*

3. Pull on the strap (*retzua*) until the *tefillin* are tightly bound to your arm. Practice makes perfect; eventually you will learn how to keep everything from slipping. Don't let the knot loosen while you wind the rest of the strap.

רְצוּעָה

4. You may want to wind the strap once around your upper arm to keep the *bayit* in place.

בַּיִת

5. Next, wind the strap seven times around your arm between your elbow and wrist. Some rabbis say that the seven times should remind us of the seven Hebrew words in the verse in Psalms, "You open Your hand and satisfy all living creatures" (145:16). Ashkenazic Jews wind the strap counterclockwise (toward their bodies), while Sephardic Jews wind it clockwise (away from their bodies). The black side of the strap should always face outward.

6. After the seventh wind, bring the strap around the outside of your hand to your palm and wrap the rest of it around the middle of your palm (i.e., the space between your thumb and index finger). Tuck the end of the strap underneath this middle coil.

19

תְּפִלִּין שֶׁל רֹאשׁ 7. Unwrap the head *tefillin* (*tefillin shel rosh*). Hold the *bayit* and place it on the top of your head above your forehead, centered between your eyes. The knot should be on the back of your head, near the nape, and the straps should be brought forward to hang down over your chest with the black side outwards. Say this blessing:

בָּרוּךְ אַתָּה יְיָ אֱלֹהֵינוּ מֶלֶךְ הָעוֹלָם אֲשֶׁר קִדְּשָׁנוּ בְּמִצְוֹתָיו וְצִוָּנוּ עַל מִצְוַת תְּפִלִּין:

Baruch atah Adonai elohaynu melech ha'olam asher kid-shanu bemitzvotav vetzivanu al mitzvat tefillin.

Praised are You, Adonai our God, Sovereign of the Universe, who has made us holy with mitzvot and instructed us concerning the precept of *tefillin*.

ד
שַׁדַּי 8. Unwind the part of the strap coiled around the middle of your palm. According to Ashkenazic custom, wrap the strap three times around your middle finger, once around the lower part of that finger, and once around its middle, and one joining the two strap loops. This forms the Hebrew letter "dalet", the second letter of *Shaddai* (Almighty God). Then quote this verse:

וְאֵרַשְׂתִּיךְ לִי לְעוֹלָם. וְאֵרַשְׂתִּיךְ לִי בְּצֶדֶק וּבְמִשְׁפָּט וּבְחֶסֶד וּבְרַחֲמִים: וְאֵרַשְׂתִּיךְ לִי בֶּאֱמוּנָה, וְיָדַעַתְּ אֶת־יְיָ:

Ve'ayrastich lee l'olam ve'ayrastich lee betzedek u'vmishpat u'vchesed u'vrachamim ve'ayrastich lee be'emunah veyada'at et Adonai.

I will betroth you to Me forever. I will betroth you to Me with righteousness, with justice, with kindness, and with compassion. I will betroth you to Me with faithfulness, and you shall know God (Hosea 2:21).

9. Bring the remainder of the strap under your ring finger and over the outside of the hand, forming a "V". Then wind the strap once again around the middle of the palm, forming the Hebrew letter "shin" which is the first letter of *Shaddai* (Almighty God).

שׁ

10. To take the *tefillin* off, reverse the order. First, take off the *dalet* and *shin* on your hand. Next, take off the *shel rosh* and wrap its straps. Unwind the strap of the *shel yad* and wrap the straps. There is no single way of wrapping the *tefillin*. Just try to neatly wrap the straps around the *bayit* of the *shel yad* and *shel rosh*. ד ש

Things to remember:

1. *Tefillin* are only worn during the *Shacharit* (morning) service. Traditionally, only boys who reach the age of Bar Mitzvah wear *tefillin*. Some girls who reach the age of Bat Mitzvah also choose to wear *tefillin*.

2. *Tefillin* are not worn on Shabbat or major festivals, since holidays themselves are a sign of a person's relationship with God. *Tefillin* have become a sign of one's connection with God on ordinary days.

3. The *tallit* is always put on before *tefillin*, because it is worn every day of the year while *tefillin* are worn only on ordinary days.

4. Some people follow the custom of touching the *batim* (plural of *bayit*) with their fingers and bringing their fingers to their lips as a kiss when they say, "bind them for a sign" during the *Shema Yisrael* prayer in the morning.

Key words and phrases:

Bayit בַּיִת. The box of the *tefillin* containing the parchment.
Giddin גִידִין. Thread made from the fibers of the hip muscles of kosher animals; used for sewing closed the *bayit*.
Kesher קֶשֶׁר. *Tefillin* knot.
Maabarta מַעֲבָּרְתָּא. Leather piece that protrudes from the back of the *bayit* through which the strap is passed.
Phylacteries תְּפִלִּין. From the Greek word meaning an amulet; the common English name for *tefillin*.
Retzua רְצוּעָה. Leather strap.

Shaddai שַׁדָי. Ancient name for God. The *tefillin* straps wound around the arm and fingers form the Hebrew letters *shin* שׁ and *dalet* ד. The *kesher* (knot) next to the *bayit* of the hand *tefillin* represents the Hebrew letter *yod* י. When, combined, the *shin* שׁ, *dalet* ד, and *yod* י spell out the word *Shaddai,* שַׁדָי one of God's oldest names.

Shin שׁ (Hebrew letter). Two letter *shins,* one with three branches (   ) and the other with four (   ) are on the *tefillin shel rosh*. Some say that the three-branched *shin* symbolizes the three patriarchs, Abraham, Isaac, and Jacob. The four-branched *shin* is a reminder of the four matriarchs Sarah, Rebecca, Rachel, and Leah. The mystics say that the meaning of the four-branched *shin* will only be revealed to us when the Messiah comes.

Tefillah תְּפִלָה. Singular of *tefillin*.

Tefillah shel rosh תְּפִלָה שֶׁל רֹאשׁ. The *tefillin* placed on the head.

Tefillah shel yad תְּפִלָה שֶׁל יָד. The *tefillin* placed on the upper arm and wound around the hand.

Titura תִּיתוֹרָא. The square base of the *bayit*.

If you want to know more:

Encyclopaedia Judaica (Jerusalem, 1973) 15:898–903.
Aryeh Kaplan, *Tefillin* (New York, 1975).
Richard Siegel, Michael Strassfeld, and Sharon Strassfeld.
  The First Jewish Catalogue (Philadelphia, 1973).

More particulars:

I. *Adjusting the tefillin knot*
    If your *tefillin* headband is too large for you, and you want to make it smaller, here is what you do.
    1. Notice that the knot has four quarters. Take hold of the lower left quarter and pull it out.
    2. Now you have a loop hanging down.
    3. Take hold of the upper right quarter and loosen it a little. Pull it from the back, taking in the lower left loop you had before. Keep pulling until the lower loop disappears.

4. Now you have a loop left on top. To make this loop disappear, just pull down on the trailing portion of the right *retzua*.

If your headband is too small and you wish to make it larger, here is what you do:

1. Notice that the *kesher* (knot) has four quarters. Each quarter is really a tight loop.

2. Take hold of the upper right quarter and pull it out into a loose loop.

3. Now pull out the lower left quarter of the knot until you get a loop.

4. Now to make the lower loop disappear, simply pull on the portion of the strap which extends upward.

Now your *kesher* is back to normal again, and your headband is enlarged. Readjust the knot so that it is in the center of the loop which goes around your head.

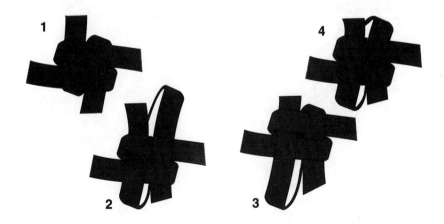

II. *Two Kinds of Tefillin:* Rashi *Tefillin*/Rabbenu Tam *Tefillin.*

There are two kinds of *tefillin:* Rashi *tefillin* and Rabbenu Tam *tefillin*. Most Jews use Rashi *tefillin*. Some put both on at different times of the morning prayers, usually putting on Rabbenu Tam *tefillin* after *Shemoneh Esray* and reciting *Shema* a second time. The two differ only in the order of the passages on the parchment in the *tefillin shel rosh*. Rashi's order follows the order in which the paragraphs appear in the Bible: Exodus 13:1–10, 13:11–16; Deuteronomy 6:4–9, 11:13–21. Rabbenu Tam (Rashi's grandson), reorders the place of the last two paragraphs, placing Deuteronomy 11:13–21 before Deuteronomy 6:4–9.

Putting on a Tallit
טַלִּית

The source:

וַיֹּאמֶר יְיָ אֶל־מֹשֶׁה לֵּאמֹר: דַּבֵּר אֶל־בְּנֵי יִשְׂרָאֵל וְאָמַרְתָּ אֲלֵהֶם
וְעָשׂוּ לָהֶם צִיצִת עַל־כַּנְפֵי בִגְדֵיהֶם לְדֹרֹתָם וְנָתְנוּ עַל־צִיצִת
הַכָּנָף פְּתִיל תְּכֵלֶת: וְהָיָה לָכֶם לְצִיצִת וּרְאִיתֶם אֹתוֹ וּזְכַרְתֶּם
אֶת־כָּל־מִצְוֹת יְיָ וַעֲשִׂיתֶם אֹתָם וְלֹא תָתוּרוּ אַחֲרֵי לְבַבְכֶם
וְאַחֲרֵי עֵינֵיכֶם אֲשֶׁר־אַתֶּם זֹנִים אַחֲרֵיהֶם: לְמַעַן תִּזְכְּרוּ וַעֲ־
שִׂיתֶם אֶת־כָּל־מִצְוֹתָי וִהְיִיתֶם קְדֹשִׁים לֵאלֹהֵיכֶם: אֲנִי יְיָ אֱלֹ־
הֵיכֶם אֲשֶׁר הוֹצֵאתִי אֶתְכֶם מֵאֶרֶץ מִצְרַיִם לִהְיוֹת לָכֶם לֵאלֹ־
הִים אֲנִי יְיָ אֱלֹהֵיכֶם:

"And God said to Moses: Instruct the people of Israel
that in every generation they shall put fringes on the
corners of their garments and bind a thread of blue
to the fringe of each corner. Looking upon it, you
will always be reminded of all the mitzvot of God and
fulfill them and not be led astray by your eyes. Then
you will remember and observe all of My mitzvot and
be holy before your God. I am Adonai your God, who
brought you out of the land of Egypt to be your God.
I, Adonai, am your God" (Num. 15:37–41).

What you need to know:

1. Before putting on the *tallit,* inspect the *tzitzit* (fringes)
   to be sure that they are intact and correct. Some
   people then say these verses from the Book of Psalms,
   to heighten their desire to put on a *tallit:* "Bless my
   soul, Adonai. You are very great, clothed in glory and
   majesty, wrapped in a robe of light. You spread the
   heavens like a tent cloth" (Ps. 104:1–2).

2. Next, hold the *tallit* and spread it open with the *atara*
   (neckpiece) facing you. Say this *beracha:*

בָּרוּךְ אַתָּה יְיָ אֱלֹהֵינוּ מֶלֶךְ הָעוֹלָם אֲשֶׁר קִדְּשָׁנוּ בְּמִצְוֹתָיו
וְצִוָּנוּ לְהִתְעַטֵּף בַּצִּיצִית:

Baruch atah Adonai elohaynu melech ha'olam asher kid-shanu bemitzvotav vetzivanu l'hitatef ba'tzitzit.

Praised are You, Adonai our God, Sovereign of the Universe, who has made us holy with mitzvot and instructed us to wrap ourselves with *tzitzit.*

Some now have the custom of kissing each end of the neckpiece, after the blessing before putting on the *tallit.* Others wrap their head briefly with the *tallit* for a moment of meditation.

3. Then bring the *tallit* around behind you and have it rest on your shoulders.

Things to remember:

1. The *tallit* is worn during the *Shacharit* (morning) service. (The exception to this is on Yom Kippur. At the *Kol Nidre* service, a *tallit* is worn in the evening and all day on Yom Kippur. Also, on Tisha B'av, it is worn only in the afternoon.) Traditionally, only boys who reach the age of Bar Mitzvah, or married men, wear a *tallit.* Some girls who reach the age of Bat Mitzvah also choose to wear a *tallit.*

2. A *tallit* is always put on before *tefillin,* because it is worn every day of the year while *tefillin* are not worn on Shabbat and holidays.

3. Most traditional boys and men wear a *tallit katan* (a small *tallit*) under their shirts all day and a large *tallit* just for morning prayers.

4. Many people follow the custom of bringing the *tzitzit* to their lips and kissing them each time the word *tzitzit* is mentioned when reading the third paragraph of the *Shema* (Num. 15:37–41).

Key words and phrases:

Atara עֲטָרָה. The crown or neckpiece of the *tallit*.

Shamash שַׁמָשׁ. The longer strand in a *tzitzit* making kit used for the winding.

Tallit katan טַלִּית קָטָן. Small *tallit* worn under the clothing during the day.

Techelet תְּכֵלֶת. The original blue color which was used in the making of *tzitzit*.

Tzitzit צִיצִית. Fringes on the four corners of the *tallit*.

If you want to know more:

Encyclopaedia Judaica (Jerusalem, 1971) 15:743.

Alfred J. Kolatch, *The Jewish Home Advisor* (Middle Village, N.Y., 1990).

Richard Siegel, Michael Strassfeld, and Sharon Strassfeld, *The First Jewish Catalogue* (Philadelphia, 1973).

More particulars:

I. *Tying the tzitzit*

1. Buy a *tzitzit*—making kit at your local Judaica store. There are sixteen strands in the pack. Separate them into four groups with one long strand and three short in each.

2. Even up the four strands at one end and push the group through one of the corners of the *tallit*.

3. Even up seven of the eight strands (the original four were doubled) and leave the extra length of the *shamash* (the longest strand) hanging to one side.

4. With four strands in one hand and four in the other, make a double knot near the edge of the material. Take the *shamash* and wind it around the other seven strands in a spiral seven times. Make another double knot.

5. Next, spiral the *shamash* eight times around and make another knot.

6. Spiral the *shamash* eleven times around and make a double knot.

7. Finally, spiral the *shamash* thirteen times around and make one final double knot.

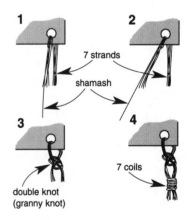

II. *Symbolism of the tzitzit*

1. In *gematria,* (Jewish numerology) the Hebrew word *tzitzit* (צִיצִית) has the number value of 600. In addition, there are eight strands plus five double knots for each *tzitzit.* This totals 613, which is the exact number of commandments in the Torah.

2. The wound spirals in each *tzitzit* are seven, eight, eleven, and thirteen. Seven plus eight equals fifteen, which in *gematria* is equal to the letters *yod* י and *hey* ה—the first two letters of God's name. Eleven is the equivalent of the Hebrew letters *vav* ו and *hey* ה—the last two letters of God's name. The combined total of twenty-six is representative of the four-letter name of God יהוה. Thirteen is the number value of the Hebrew word *echad* (אֶחָד), which means One. Thus, to look at the *tzitzit* is to always be reminded that God is One (יהוה אֶחָד).

III. *How to put on a Tallit*

(1) A *tallit* worn fully over back and shoulders. (2) Folding the *tallit* over the shoulders. (3) A *tallit* folded back over the shoulders—a side view. (4) A front view.

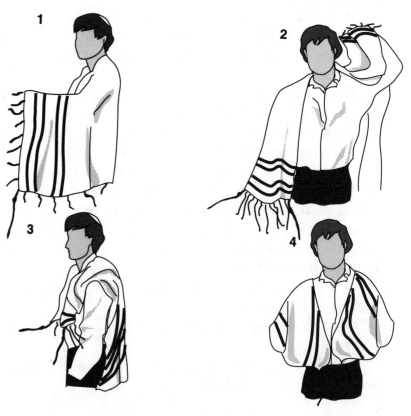

Baking and Braiding a Challah for Shabbat
חַלָּה

The source:

Taking challah is from Numbers 15:19–21, Mishnah Challah 1:1. Braids are mystical; they are from the hair of
the Sabbath bride.

What you need to know:

1. Dissolve 2 packages granulated yeast in 2 cups tepid
   water. Add 1/2 cup sugar. Set aside.

2. Mix together 7 cups flour and 2 teaspoons salt. Add
   1/3 cup oil, 2 lightly beaten eggs, and the yeast
   mixture. Combine well.

3. Knead on a floured board until smooth and silky.
   Add 1/2 cup golden raisins. Place in well-oiled bowl;
   cover and allow to rise in a warm, draft-free place
   until double in size, about 2 hours.

4. Punch down and allow to rise again, about 1 hour.

5. Divide dough and braid into 2 loaves. Place on cookie
   sheet and allow to rise 2 hours.
   While you are preparing the challah dough, separate a small piece and toss it into the oven. This
   is a symbol of contemporary sacrifice and also a
   reminder of the part of the challah that was given to
   the priests in the ancient Temple. When you do this,
   recite the following blessing:

בָּרוּךְ אַתָּה יְיָ אֱלֹהֵינוּ מֶלֶךְ הָעוֹלָם אֲשֶׁר קִדְּשָׁנוּ בְּמִצְוֹתָיו
וְצִוָּנוּ לְהַפְרִישׁ חַלָּה.

Baruch atah Adonai elohaynu melech ha'olam asher kidshanu bemitzvotav vetzivanu le'hafrish challah.

Praised are you, Adonai our God, Sovereign of the Universe, who has made us holy with mitzvot and instructed us to separate challah.

To braid, divide the dough into three parts. Roll each into a long snake of even thickness. Then pinch together the ends and braid as you do hair. As an alternative, overlap braids in the other and braid toward the end.

6. Brush with egg wash and sprinkle with sesame seeds. Bake in oven at 350° for 25 minutes.

7. After baking, breaking, and washing your hands, place the two *challot* on the challah board, lay all ten fingers on the *challot,* and say the following:

בָּרוּךְ אַתָּה יְיָ אֱלֹהֵינוּ מֶלֶךְ הָעוֹלָם הַמּוֹצִיא לֶחֶם מִן הָאָרֶץ.

Baruch atah Adonai elohaynu melech ha'olam hamotzi lechem min ha'aretz.

Praised are You, Adonai our God, Sovereign of the Universe, who brings forth bread from the earth.

Things to remember:

1. Only bread from these grains needs to be "separated" (as challah): wheat, barley, maize (corn), spelt, and oats.

2. If you forget to "separate" the challah before it is baked, it can be broken off and burnt later.

3. Cover the knives on the table before saying the blessing. Remember, the table has become the altar and knives were not permitted there (take a look at Isaiah 2:4).

4. Since the altar was made from hewn stones, some people tear the *challot* apart—instead of using a knife—because a knife is a weapon of war (take a look at Exodus 20:22).

5. After the blessing, before eating the challah, salt the bread (just a little) as a reminder of the sacrifice at the Temple. This also reveals that "by the sweat of your brow shall you get bread to eat" (Gen. 3:19).

6. Braided *challot* are used on Shabbat. Round *challot* are used on festivals, especially Rosh Hashana. Some communities serve *challot* shaped like birds on Rosh Hashana to show that God's mercy extends even to little birds.

7. The poppy or sesame seeds represent the manna which fell in the desert.

Key words and phrases:

Challah חַלָה (plural, *challot* חַלּוֹת). Dough.

If you want to know more:

Freda Reider, *The Hallah Book* (Hoboken, N.J. 1988).

Lifting and Tying a Torah
הַגְבָּהָה וּגְלִילָה

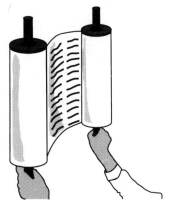

The source:

1. Babylonian Talmud, Sofrim 14:14.
2. Orach Chayim 134:2.

What you need to know:

עֲלִיּוֹת   Generally, both of these *aliyot* (Torah honors, from the word which means "to go up") are called at the same time following the reading of the Torah.

הַגְבָּהָה   1. For *hagbahah* (lifting), unroll the Torah scroll to a width of three columns.

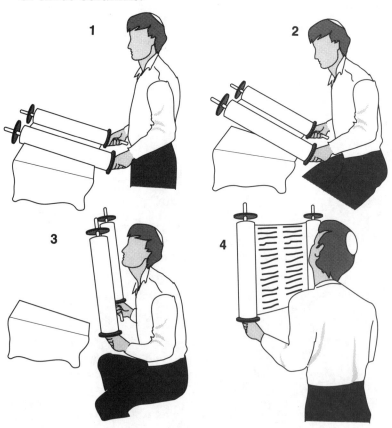

2. Slide the Torah scroll down the reading table so that the bottom rollers are off the table.

3. Hold the rollers tightly. Using the table for leverage, bend your knees and push down on the bottom ends of the rollers.

4. Lift the scroll high above your head. Be careful.

5. Turn around so that the inside of the scroll—the writing—can be seen by the congregation.

6. After the congregation has chanted *Vezot ha-Torah,* sit down in the chair provided for you. Here, the one doing *gelilah* takes over. Just help.

וְזֹאת הַתּוֹרָה
גְּלִילָה

1. For *gelilah* (rolling and tying the Torah), hold the top of the Torah rollers and roll the scroll together (with the steady help of the person who did *hagbahah*).

2. When it is together, put the Genesis side (your left side) of the roller over the other side.

3. Take the *avnet* or wimpel (binder) and fasten it around the front of the Torah.

אַבְנֵט

4. A sash is tied in a bow. A wimpel is tucked at the end, after it has been wrapped.

5. Cover the Torah with its mantle/cover, making sure the decoration faces front.

6. Then put the breastplate and pointer back on. (Some synagogues wait to finish until after the Haftarah is read.)

Now the *gelilah* person sits down in his/her seat, after shaking hands. The *hagbahah* person will remain and hold the Torah in his/her lap until the rest of the folks are ready to return it to the ark.

Things to remember:

יַשֶׁר כֹּחַ
בָּרוּךְ תִּהְיֶה

1. Shake hands with everyone on the *bimah* after you have finished your aliyah. People will say, *yeshar koach.* Remember to respond, *baruch tihyeh.*

Key words and phrases:

Avnet אַבְנֵט. *Torah binder, sometimes called a wimpel.*
Choshen חוֹשֶׁן. Silver shield breastplate over the front of the Torah which remind us of the High Priest's breastplate in the Temple.
Me'il מְעִיל. Torah mantle/cover.
Rimmon(im) רִימוֹן. From the Hebrew word for pomegranates, which were used to adorn Torah scrolls, generally silver objects with bells that are placed on top of each of the Torah rollers.
Yad יָד. Pointer used to point to words in the Torah during reading.

If you want to know more:

Hayim Donin, *To Pray as a Jew* (New York, 1980).

Chanting the Haftarah Blessings and Haftarah Trope
בִּרְכוֹת הַהַפְטָרָה וְטַעֲמֵי הַמִקְרָא

The source:

The Levites used hand-signs which represented specific melodies when they were teaching the Torah in public. These were eventually adapted for the Haftarah as well.

What you need to know:

1. The Haftarah (a section from one of the books of the Prophets) is chanted in synagogues on Shabbat and festivals.

הַפְטָרָה

2. Each Haftarah consists of Hebrew words with musical notations, known as *trop* or *ta'amei hamikra* in Hebrew. These signs tell us how to sing the words and phrases in the Haftarah.

טַעֲמֵי הַמִקְרָא

3. There is a blessing before every Haftarah that is chanted, and several blessings after every Haftarah that are also chanted.

4. Here are the blessings before and after the Haftarah with the accompanying music (used, with permission, from Samuel Rosenbaum's *Guide to Haftarah Chanting* [KTAV Publishing House, 1973]).

Blessing before the Haftarah

בָּרוּךְ אַתָּה יְיָ, אֱלֹהֵינוּ מֶלֶךְ הָעוֹלָם, אֲשֶׁר בָּחַר בִּנְבִיאִים
טוֹבִים, וְרָצָה בְדִבְרֵיהֶם, הַנֶּאֱמָרִים בֶּאֱמֶת: בָּרוּךְ אַתָּה יְיָ,
הַבּוֹחֵר בַּתּוֹרָה, וּבְמשֶׁה עַבְדּוֹ, וּבְיִשְׂרָאֵל עַמּוֹ, וּבִנְבִיאֵי הָאֱמֶת
וָצֶדֶק:

35

The blessings which follow the Haftarah are chanted, not according to *trop* markings (none are given), but to a traditional tune. This tune may vary from community to community, but, generally speaking, the version notated below is well-known in most American congregations.

Blessings after concluding the Haftarah

בָּרוּךְ אַתָּה יְיָ, אֱלֹהֵינוּ מֶלֶךְ הָעוֹלָם, צוּר כָּל הָעוֹלָמִים, צַדִּיק
בְּכָל־הַדּוֹרוֹת, הָאֵל הַנֶּאֱמָן, הָאוֹמֵר וְעוֹשֶׂה, הַמְדַבֵּר וּמְקַיֵּם,
שֶׁכָּל דְּבָרָיו אֱמֶת וָצֶדֶק:
נֶאֱמָן אַתָּה הוּא יְיָ אֱלֹהֵינוּ, וְנֶאֱמָנִים דְּבָרֶיךָ, וְדָבָר אֶחָד
מִדְּבָרֶיךָ, אָחוֹר לֹא־יָשׁוּב רֵיקָם, כִּי אֵל מֶלֶךְ נֶאֱמָן וְרַחֲמָן
אָתָּה: בָּרוּךְ אַתָּה יְיָ, הָאֵל הַנֶּאֱמָן בְּכָל־דְּבָרָיו:
רַחֵם עַל־צִיּוֹן כִּי הִיא בֵּית חַיֵּינוּ, וְלַעֲלוּבַת נֶפֶשׁ תּוֹשִׁיעַ בִּמְהֵרָה
בְיָמֵינוּ: בָּרוּךְ אַתָּה יְיָ, מְשַׂמֵּחַ צִיּוֹן בְּבָנֶיהָ:

שַׂמְּחֵנוּ יְיָ אֱלֹהֵינוּ, בְּאֵלִיָּהוּ הַנָּבִיא עַבְדֶּךָ, וּבְמַלְכוּת בֵּית דָּוִד
מְשִׁיחֶךָ, בִּמְהֵרָה יָבֹא וְיָגֵל לִבֵּנוּ, עַל כִּסְאוֹ לֹא יֵשֶׁב זָר, וְלֹא
יִנְחֲלוּ עוֹד אֲחֵרִים אֶת כְּבוֹדוֹ, כִּי בְּשֵׁם קָדְשְׁךָ נִשְׁבַּעְתָּ לּוֹ,
שֶׁלֹּא יִכְבֶּה נֵרוֹ לְעוֹלָם וָעֶד: בָּרוּךְ אַתָּה יְיָ, מָגֵן דָּוִד:
עַל הַתּוֹרָה, וְעַל הָעֲבוֹדָה, וְעַל הַנְּבִיאִים, וְעַל יוֹם הַשַּׁבָּת הַזֶּה,
שֶׁנָּתַתָּ לָנוּ יְיָ אֱלֹהֵינוּ לִקְדֻשָּׁה וְלִמְנוּחָה לְכָבוֹד וּלְתִפְאָרֶת:

עַל־הַכֹּל יְיָ אֱלֹהֵינוּ, אֲנַחְנוּ מוֹדִים לָךְ וּמְבָרְכִים אוֹתָךְ, יִתְבָּרַךְ
שִׁמְךָ בְּפִי כָּל־חַי תָּמִיד לְעוֹלָם וָעֶד: בָּרוּךְ אַתָּה יְיָ, מְקַדֵּשׁ
הַשַּׁבָּת:

* On Sabbath Chol Hamoed Pesach the same *berachot* are chanted as on an ordinary Sabbath.

38

(6)

Al ha-kol ___ A-do-nai e-lo-he-nu a-

nach-nu mo-dim lach ___ u-mi-var-chim o-tach, ___ yit-ba-rech

shim-cha be-fee ___ kol chai ta-mid li-o-lam ___ va-

ed. Ba-ruch a-ta A-do-nai m-ka-desh ha-sha-bat.

Haftarah *Trop*

Mer-cha ___ tip-cha mu-nach et-nach-ta ___

Ma-pach ___ pash-ta ___ mu-nach ___ ka-ton ___

Dar-gah ___ t'-vir ___

Ger-sha-yim ___ [mu-nach] r'-vi-i ___

Kad-ma az-lah ___ [*only when followed by an azlah]

T'-li-sha g'do-lah ___ t'li-sha k'ta-nah ___

Pa-zer ___ [mu-nach] zar-kah ___ [mu-nach] se-gol

39

Key words and phrases:

Haftarah הַפְטָרָה. From the Hebrew word meaning "conclusion," specifically refers to the section from the Prophets read on Shabbat and festivals.

Ta'amei hamikra טַעֲמֵי הַמִּקְרָא. Musical signs for the reading of the Torah, Hebrew *trop*; from the Yiddish for "musical sign," cantillation marks.

If you want to know more:

Richard Neumann, *The Roots of Biblical Chants* (New York, 1982).

Samuel Rosenbaum, *A Guide to Haftarah Chanting* (New York, 1973).

Chanting the Torah
טַעֲמֵי הַמִקְרָא

The source:

The Levites used hand-signs which represented specific melodies when they were teaching the Torah in public.

What you need to know:

1. The Torah (the Five Books of Moses written on parchment) is chanted in the synagogue on Mondays, Thursdays, Shabbat festivals and fast days.

2. The chanting of the Hebrew words in the Torah are practised using a book called a *Tikkun*. This book contains the printed text with vowels and musical notations known as *trop* or *ta'amei hamikra* in Hebrew. This appears alongside the text of the Torah. The musical signs tell how to sing the words and phrases in the Torah.

3. The chanter of the Torah uses a Torah pointer, called a *yad* (in the shape of a hand) with which to follow the words.

4. There are no vowels, *trop* or punctuation marks in the Torah. The reader must have a good memory in addition to some singing skills.

Hand Signs for Torah Reading

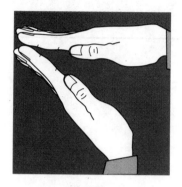

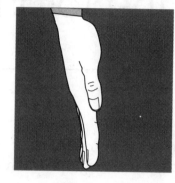

R' - vi - i _____

Ma - pach _____

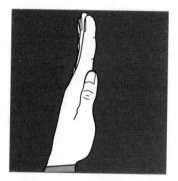

Tip-cha

Mer-cha

Pash - ta

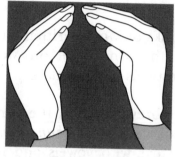

Et - nach - ta _____

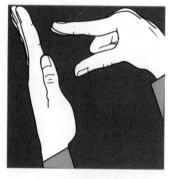

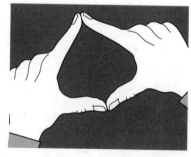

Sof   pa - suk _____

Za - kef   ga - dol _____

42

Table of Torah Trop Melodies

Key words and phrases:

Tikkun תִּקּוּן. A special book used to prepare for the reading of the Torah because it contains the printed text with vowels parallel to the text without vowels.

Yad יָד. A pointer used for the reading of the Torah so that one does not touch the Torah scroll itself.

If you want to know more:

Richard Neumann, *The Roots of Biblical Chants* (New York, 1982).

Samuel Rosenbaum, *A Guide to Torah Reading* (New York, 1983).

Samuel Rosenbaum, *To Live as a Jew* (New York, 1969).

Birkat Ha-Gomel
בִּרְכַּת הַגּוֹמֵל

The source:

Psalm 107; Babylonian Talmud, Berachot 54b.

What you need to know:

Just say the following, after an *aliyah* in a public Torah reading:

בָּרוּךְ אַתָּה יְיָ אֱלֹהֵינוּ מֶלֶךְ הָעוֹלָם הַגּוֹמֵל לְחַיָּבִים טוֹבוֹת שֶׁגְּמָלַנִי כָּל טוֹב:

Baruch atah Adonai elohaynu melech ha'olam hagomel lechayavim tovot she'gemalani kol tov.

Praised are You, Adonai our God, Sovereign of the Universe, who bestows favor on those who do not deserve it, just as You have bestowed favor on me.

Things to remember:

1. Say *Birkat Ha-Gomel* after you have returned home from a long trip, recovered from a serious illness, escaped disaster (including an automobile accident), or been released from an imprisonment! Women say it after having a baby too.

2. After you recite your blessing, the congregation will respond:

מִי שֶׁגְּמָלְךָ כָּל טוֹב הוּא יִגְמָלְךָ כָּל טוֹב סֶלָה:

Mi shegemalcha kol tov hu yegemalcha kol tov selah.

May the One who has shown you every kindness continue to deal kindly with you.

Key words and phrases:

Gomel גוֹמֵל. A person who has been "given a break" and saved from a life—threatening situation.

If you want to know more:

Isaac Klein, *A Guide to Jewish Religious Practice* (New York, 1979).
Richard Siegel, Michael Strassfeld, and Sharon Strassfeld, *The First Jewish Catalogue* (Philadelphia, 1973).

Night Prayer—
Keriat Shema Al Hameeta
קְרִיאַת שְׁמַע עַל הַמִּטָה

The source:

וְשִׁנַּנְתָּם לְבָנֶיךָ וְדִבַּרְתָּ בָּם בְּשִׁבְתְּךָ בְּבֵיתֶךָ וּבְלֶכְתְּךָ בַדֶּרֶךְ וּבְשָׁכְבְּךָ וּבְקוּמֶךָ:

"And you shall speak of them when you are sitting in your home, when you go on a journey, when you lie down" (Deut. 6:7).

Also see Babylonian Talmud, Berachot 60b.

What you need to know:

1. Recited before retiring:

בָּרוּךְ אַתָּה יְיָ אֱלֹהֵינוּ מֶלֶךְ הָעוֹלָם הַמַּפִּיל חֶבְלֵי שֵׁנָה עַל עֵינַי וּתְנוּמָה עַל עַפְעַפָּי: וִיהִי רָצוֹן מִלְפָנֶיךָ יְיָ אֱלֹהַי וֵאלֹהֵי אֲבוֹתַי שֶׁתַּשְׁכִּיבֵנִי לְשָׁלוֹם וְתַעֲמִידֵנִי לְשָׁלוֹם וְאַל יְבַהֲלוּנִי רַעְיוֹנַי וַחֲלוֹמוֹת רָעִים וְהִרְהוּרִים רָעִים וּתְהִי מִטָּתִי שְׁלֵמָה לְפָנֶיךָ: וְהָאֵר עֵינַי פֶּן אִישַׁן הַמָּוֶת, כִּי אַתָּה הַמֵּאִיר לְאִישׁוֹן בַּת עָיִן: בָּרוּךְ אַתָּה יְיָ הַמֵּאִיר לָעוֹלָם כֻּלוֹ בִּכְבוֹדוֹ:

Blessed are You, Adonai, Sovereign of the Universe, who closes my eyes in sleep and my eyelids in slumber. May it be Your desire, God of my ancestors, to grant that I lie down in peace and that I rise up in peace. Let my thoughts not upset me nor evil dreams. May my family be perfect in Your sight. Grant me light, lest I sleep the sleep of death. It is You that gives light to the eyes. Praised are You, God, whose majesty gives light to the entire world.

שְׁמַע יִשְׂרָאֵל יְיָ אֱלֹהֵינוּ יְיָ אֶחָד:

Shema Yisrael Adonai elohaynu Adonai echad.

בָּרוּךְ שֵׁם כְּבוֹד מַלְכוּתוֹ לְעוֹלָם וָעֶד:

Baruch shem kevod malchuto le'olam va'ed.

47

2.

וְאָהַבְתָּ אֵת יְיָ אֱלֹהֶיךָ בְּכָל־לְבָבְךָ וּבְכָל־נַפְשְׁךָ וּבְכָל־מְאֹדֶךָ: וְהָיוּ הַדְּבָרִים הָאֵלֶּה אֲשֶׁר אָנֹכִי מְצַוְּךָ הַיּוֹם עַל־לְבָבֶךָ: וְשִׁנַּנְתָּם לְבָנֶיךָ וְדִבַּרְתָּ בָּם בְּשִׁבְתְּךָ בְּבֵיתֶךָ וּבְלֶכְתְּךָ בַדֶּרֶךְ וּבְשָׁכְבְּךָ וּבְקוּמֶךָ: וּקְשַׁרְתָּם לְאוֹת עַל־יָדֶךָ וְהָיוּ לְטֹטָפֹת בֵּין עֵינֶיךָ: וּכְתַבְתָּם עַל־מְזוּזֹת בֵּיתֶךָ וּבִשְׁעָרֶיךָ:

Hear, O Israel, Adonai is our God, Adonai is One. Praised be God's majestic reputation forever and ever. Love Adonai your God with all your heart, soul, and might. And these words which I command you today shall be in your heart. Teach them carefully to your children, and speak of them when you sit in your home, when you go on a journey, when you lie down, and when you arise. Bind them as a sign on your hand and they shall be for frontlets between your eyes. Inscribe them on the doorposts of your house and on your gates (Deut. 4:6–9).

Things to remember:

Don't forget to say the Shema each night before going to bed, the last thing you do.

Key words and phrases:

Ayin עַיִן. (plural, *anayim* עֵינַיִם). Eye.
Sheynah שֵׁינָה. Sleep.

If you want to know more:

Haim Donin, *To Pray as a Jew* (New York, 1980).
Isaac Klein, *A Guide to Jewish Religious Practice* (New York, 1979).
Meir Zlotowitz and Nosson Scherman, *Shema Yisrael* (New York, 1982).

Key words and phrases:

Hadlakat nerot הַדְלָקַת נֵרוֹת. The lighting of candles.
Ner נֵר. (plural, *nerot* נֵרוֹת,) candle.

If you want to know more:

Malka Drucker, *Shabbat, a Peaceful Island* (New York, 1983).
Ronald H. Isaacs, *Shabbat Delight* (Hoboken, N.J., 1987).

How to Light the Sabbath Candles
הַדְלָקַת נֵרוֹת

The sources:

Exodus 20:8; Deuteronomy 5:12.

זָכוֹר (שָׁמוֹר) אֶת יוֹם הַשַׁבָּת לְקַדְשׁוֹ.

Remember (observe) the Sabbath day to keep it holy.

What you need to know:

1. Candles are lit at between 1 1/2 hours and 18 minutes prior to sunset (according to halacha).

2. Light the candles.

3. Draw your hands around the candles and toward your face from one to seven times (three times is most common).

4. Cover your eyes with your hands and say the following blessing at the same time:

בָּרוּךְ אַתָּה יְיָ אֱלֹהֵינוּ מֶלֶךְ הָעוֹלָם אֲשֶׁר קִדְשָׁנוּ בְּמִצְוֹתָיו
וְצִוָּנוּ לְהַדְלִיק נֵר שֶׁל שַׁבָּת:

Baruch atah Adonai elohaynu melech ha'olam asher kidshanu bemitzvotav vetzivanu l'hadlik ner shel Shabbat.

Praised are You, Adonai our God, Sovereign of the Universe, who makes us holy with mitzvot and instructs us to kindle the lights of Shabbat.

The blessing for Yom Tov is:

בָּרוּךְ אַתָּה יְיָ אֱלֹהֵינוּ מֶלֶךְ הָעוֹלָם אֲשֶׁר קִדְשָׁנוּ בְּמִצְוֹתָיו
וְצִוָּנוּ לְהַדְלִיק נֵר שֶׁל (שַׁבָּת וְשֶׁל) יוֹם טוֹב:

49

*Baruch atah Adonai elohaynu melech ha'olam asher kid-
shanu bemitzvotav vetzivanu l'hadlik ner shel (Shabbat
v'shel) Yom Tov.*

Praised are You, Adonai our God, Sovereign of the
Universe, who makes us holy with mitzvot and in-
structs us to kindle the lights of (Shabbat and) Yom
Tov.

The blessing for Yom Kippur is:

בָּרוּךְ אַתָּה יְיָ אֱלֹהֵינוּ מֶלֶךְ הָעוֹלָם אֲשֶׁר קִדְּשָׁנוּ בְּמִצְוֹתָיו
וְצִוָּנוּ לְהַדְלִיק נֵר שֶׁל (שַׁבָּת וְשֶׁל) יוֹם הַכִּפּוּרִים:

*Baruch atah Adonai elohaynu melech ha'olam asher kid-
shanu bemitzvotav vetzivanu l'hadlik ner shel (Shabbat
v'shel) Yom ha-Kippurim.*

Praised are You, Adonai our God, Sovereign of the
Universe, who makes us holy with mitzvot and in-
structs us to kindle the lights of (Shabbat and) the
Day of Atonement.

Things to remember:

1. Candles are lit for the sake of *shalom bayit* and *oneg
   Shabbat*.

2. Traditionally, women light the candles, but men are
   encouraged to do so.

3. While you are required to light two candles, it is permitted to light more. Families of Eastern European
   heritage often light more, often one for each child.
   This is an interpretation of the verse "God blessed
   the Sabbath day." How? With light. Once you have
   established a pattern, continue to light that number
   each week.

4. If there are no candles available, you may say the
   blessing over electric or gas lights.

Key words and phrases:

Hadlakat nerot הַדְלָקַת נֵרוֹת. The lighting of candles.
Ner נֵר. (plural, *nerot* נֵרוֹת,) candle.

If you want to know more:

Malka Drucker, *Shabbat, a Peaceful Island* (New York, 1983).
Ronald H. Isaacs, *Shabbat Delight* (Hoboken, N.J., 1987).
Isaac Klein, *A Guide to Jewish Religious Practice* (New York, 1979).
Abraham Milgram, *The Shabbat Anthology* (Philadelphia, 1944).
Mark Dov Shapiro, *Gates of Shabbat* (New York, 1991).

How to Make Shabbat Evening Kiddush
קִדּוּשׁ לְשַׁבָּת

The source:

There are various sources, including Exodus 20:8.

זָכוֹר אֶת יוֹם הַשַּׁבָּת לְקַדְּשׁוֹ:

Remember the Sabbath Day to keep it holy.

What you need to know:

1. Raise the cup by holding it in your hand, cupped at the bottom.

2. Say the following:

וַיְכֻלּוּ הַשָּׁמַיִם וְהָאָרֶץ וְכָל־צְבָאָם: וַיְכַל אֱלֹהִים בַּיּוֹם הַשְּׁבִיעִי
מְלַאכְתּוֹ אֲשֶׁר עָשָׂה. וַיִּשְׁבֹּת בַּיּוֹם הַשְּׁבִיעִי מִכָּל־מְלַאכְתּוֹ
אֲשֶׁר עָשָׂה: וַיְבָרֶךְ אֱלֹהִים אֶת־יוֹם הַשְּׁבִיעִי וַיְקַדֵּשׁ אֹתוֹ. כִּי
בוֹ שָׁבַת מִכָּל מְלַאכְתּוֹ אֲשֶׁר־בָּרָא אֱלֹהִים לַעֲשׂוֹת:

Vayechulu hashamayim ve'ha-aretz vechol tzeva'am vayechal Elohim bayom ha-shevi'i melachto asher asah. Vayishbot bayom hashevi'i mikol melachto asher asah vayevarech Elohim et yom hashevi'i vayekadesh oto ki vo shavat mikol melachto asher bara Elohim la'asot.

Now the whole universe—sky, earth, and all their array—was completed. With the seventh day God ended the work of Creation; on the seventh day God rested with all the Divine work completed. Then God blessed the seventh day and called it holy, for with this day God had completed the work of Creation.

בָּרוּךְ אַתָּה יְיָ אֱלֹהֵינוּ מֶלֶךְ הָעוֹלָם בּוֹרֵא פְּרִי הַגָּפֶן:

Baruch atah Adonai elohaynu melech ha'olam boray pri ha-gafen.

Praised are You, Adonai our God, Sovereign of the Universe, who creates the fruit of the vine.

בָּרוּךְ אַתָּה יְיָ אֱלֹהֵינוּ מֶלֶךְ הָעוֹלָם אֲשֶׁר קִדְּשָׁנוּ בְּמִצְוֹתָיו וְרָצָה בָנוּ וְשַׁבַּת קָדְשׁוֹ בְּאַהֲבָה וּבְרָצוֹן הִנְחִילָנוּ זִכָּרוֹן לְמַעֲשֵׂה בְרֵאשִׁית. כִּי הוּא יוֹם תְּחִלָּה לְמִקְרָאֵי קֹדֶשׁ זֵכֶר לִיצִיאַת מִצְרָיִם: כִּי בָנוּ בָחַרְתָּ וְאוֹתָנוּ קִדַּשְׁתָּ מִכָּל הָעַמִּים. וְשַׁבַּת קָדְשְׁךָ בְּאַהֲבָה וּבְרָצוֹן הִנְחַלְתָּנוּ: בָּרוּךְ אַתָּה יְיָ מְקַדֵּשׁ הַשַּׁבָּת:

Baruch atah Adonai elohaynu melech ha'olam asher kidshanu bemitzvotav veratza vanu veshabbat kodsho be'ahavah u'vratzon hinchilanu zikaron le'ma'asay vereshit ki hu yom techilah lemikra'ay kodesh zecher l'tziyat mitzrayim. Ki vanu vacharta ve'otanu kidashta mikol ha'amim veshabbat kodshecha be'ahava u'vratzon hinchaltanu. Baruch atah Adonai mikadesh ha-Shabbat.

Praised are You, Adonai our God, Sovereign of the Universe, who makes us holy with mitzvot and takes delight in us. In love and favor You have made the holy Sabbath our heritage, as a reminder of the work of Creation. It is first among our sacred days, and a remembrance of the Exodus from Egypt. O God, You have chosen us and set us apart from all the peoples and in love and favor have given us the Sabbath Day in your love and favor. Praised are You Adonai for the Sabbath and its holiness.

3. Then drink the wine.

Things to remember:

1. On Shabbat morning, sing *Veshamru,* then say only the modified blessing (over wine, not over the day).

וְשָׁמְרוּ בְנֵי־יִשְׂרָאֵל אֶת־הַשַּׁבָּת, לַעֲשׂוֹת אֶת־הַשַּׁבָּת לְדֹרֹתָם בְּרִית עוֹלָם: בֵּינִי וּבֵין בְּנֵי יִשְׂרָאֵל אוֹת הִיא לְעֹלָם, כִּי־שֵׁשֶׁת יָמִים עָשָׂה יְיָ אֶת־הַשָּׁמַיִם וְאֶת־הָאָרֶץ, וּבַיּוֹם הַשְּׁבִיעִי שָׁבַת וַיִּנָּפַשׁ:

Veshamru venay Yisrael et ha-Shabbat la'asot et ha-Shabbat ledorotam berit olam baynee u'vayn b'nai Yisrael ot hee le'olam ki sheshet yamim asah Adonai et hashamayim ve'et ha-aretz u'vayom hashevi'i shavat vayinafash.

עַל כֵּן בֵּרַךְ יְיָ אֶת־יוֹם הַשַּׁבָּת וַיְקַדְּשֵׁהוּ:

Al ken berach Adonai et yom ha-Shabbat vayekadeshayu.

בָּרוּךְ אַתָּה יְיָ אֱלֹהֵינוּ מֶלֶךְ הָעוֹלָם בּוֹרֵא פְּרִי הַגָּפֶן:

Baruch atah Adonai elohaynu melech ha'olam boray pri hagafen.

2. Remember to drink the wine (before talking) after the blessing.

3. On Yom Tov, the same blessing is replaced with the following:

בָּרוּךְ אַתָּה יְיָ אֱלֹהֵינוּ מֶלֶךְ הָעוֹלָם אֲשֶׁר בָּחַר בָּנוּ מִכָּל־עָם וְרוֹמְמָנוּ מִכָּל לָשׁוֹן, וְקִדְּשָׁנוּ בְּמִצְוֹתָיו.

Baruch atah Adonai elohaynu melech ha'olam asher bachar banu mikol am ve'romimanu mikol lashon vekidshanu bemitzvatav.

Praised is Adonai our God, Sovereign of the Universe, who has chosen us from all the peoples, exalting us by making us holy with mitzvot.

וַתִּתֶּן לָנוּ יְיָ אֱלֹהֵינוּ בְּאַהֲבָה, (שַׁבָּתוֹת לִמְנוּחָה וּ) מוֹעֲדִים לְשִׂמְחָה, חַגִּים וּזְמַנִּים לְשָׂשׂוֹן, אֶת יוֹם (הַשַּׁבָּת הַזֶּה וְאֶת יוֹם)

Vatitayn lanu Adonai elohaynu b'ahavah (Shabbatot limenucha) moadim lesimcha chagim u'zmanim le'sason et yom (ha-Shabbat hazeh ve'et yom)

In Your love, Adonai our God, You have given us (Sabbaths of rest), feasts of gladness, and seasons of joy: this (Sabbath Day and this) festival of

חַג הַמַּצּוֹת הַזֶּה, זְמַן חֵרוּתֵנוּ

chag hamatzot hazeh zeman cherutaynu

Pesach—season of our freedom

חַג הַשָׁבוּעוֹת הַזֶּה, זְמַן מַתַּן תּוֹרָתֵנוּ

chag hashavuot hazeh zeman matan torahtenu

Shavuot—season of revelation

חַג הַסֻּכּוֹת הַזֶּה, זְמַן שִׂמְחָתֵנוּ

chag hasukkot hazeh zeman simchatenu

Sukkot—season of thanksgiving

הַשְׁמִינִי חַג הָעֲצֶרֶת הַזֶּה, זְמַן שִׂמְחָתֵנוּ

hashemini chag ha'atzeret hazeh–zeman simchatenu

Shemini Atzeret Simchat Torah—season of our gladness

מִקְרָא קֹדֶשׁ זֵכֶר לִיצִיאַת מִצְרָיֶם.

mikra kodesh zecher litziyat mitzrayim.

to unite in prayer and recall the Exodus from Egypt.

כִּי בָנוּ בָחַרְתָּ וְאוֹתָנוּ קִדַּשְׁתָּ מִכָּל־הָעַמִּים, (וְשַׁבָּת) וּמוֹעֲדֵי קָדְשֶׁךָ (בְּאַהֲבָה וּבְרָצוֹן) בְּשִׂמְחָה וּבְשָׂשׂוֹן הִנְחַלְתָּנוּ: בָּרוּךְ אַתָּה יְיָ מְקַדֵּשׁ (הַשַׁבָּת וְ) יִשְׂרָאֵל וְהַזְּמַנִּים:

ki vanu vacharta ve'otanu kidashta mikol ha'amim (ve-Shabbat) u'mo'aday kodshecha (be'ahavah u'vratzon) besimcha u'vesason hinchaltanu. Baruch atah Adonai mikadesh (ha-Shabbat v') Yisrael vehazemanim.

For You have chosen us from all peoples, consecrating us to Your service and giving us (the Sabbath a sign of Your love and favor, and) the Festivals, a time of gladness and joy. Praised are You, Adonai, who makes holy (the Sabbath,) the House of Israel and the Festivals.

Key words and phrases:

Kiddush קִדּוּשׁ. From the Hebrew meaning "holy" or "separate," a prayer said to sanctify time and place.

55

Kos כּוֹס. Cup.
Yayin יַיִן. Wine.

If you want to know more:

Malka Drucker, *Shabbat, a Peaceful Island* (New York, 1983).
Ronald H. Isaacs, *Shabbat Delight* (Hoboken, N.J., 1987).
Abraham Milgram, *The Shabbat Anthology* (Philadelphia, 1944).
Mark Dov Shapiro, *Gates of Shabbat* (New York, 1991).

How to Make Havdalah
הַבְדָּלָה

The source:

Various talmudic sources, including Pesachim 103b; also
Shulchan Aruch, Orach Chayim 196:1.

What you need to know:

1. Raise the wine cup and say:

הִנֵּה אֵל יְשׁוּעָתִי, אֶבְטַח וְלֹא אֶפְחָד. כִּי עָזִּי וְזִמְרָת יָהּ יְיָ,
וַיְהִי לִי לִישׁוּעָה. וּשְׁאַבְתֶּם מַיִם בְּשָׂשׂוֹן מִמַּעַיְנֵי הַיְשׁוּעָה. לַיְיָ
הַיְשׁוּעָה עַל עַמְּךָ בִרְכָתֶךָ סֶּלָה. יְיָ צְבָאוֹת עִמָּנוּ, מִשְׂגָּב לָנוּ
אֱלֹהֵי יַעֲקֹב, סֶלָה.

Behold, God is my deliverer. I trust in You and
am not afraid. For Adonai is my strength and my
stronghold, the source of my deliverance. With joy
we draw water from the wells of salvation. Adonai
brings deliverance, blessings to the people. Selah.
Adonai is a powerful God: the God of Jacob is our
stronghold.

לַיְהוּדִים הָיְתָה אוֹרָה וְשִׂמְחָה וְשָׂשׂוֹן וִיקָר. כֵּן תִּהְיֶה לָּנוּ. כּוֹס
יְשׁוּעוֹת אֶשָּׂא וּבְשֵׁם יְיָ אֶקְרָא.

Give us light and joy, gladness and honor, as in the
happiest days of Israel's past. I lift up the cup of my
salvation and call out the name of Adonai.

בָּרוּךְ אַתָּה יְיָ אֱלֹהֵינוּ מֶלֶךְ הָעוֹלָם בּוֹרֵא פְּרִי הַגָּפֶן:

*Baruch atah Adonai elohaynu melech ha'olam boray pri
ha-gafen.*

Praise are You, Adonai our God, Sovereign of the Universe, who creates the fruit of the vine.

2. Next, lift the spice box and say:

בָּרוּךְ אַתָּה יְיָ אֱלֹהֵינוּ מֶלֶךְ הָעוֹלָם בּוֹרֵא מִינֵי בְשָׂמִים:

Baruch atah Adonai elohaynu melech ha'olam boray minay vesamim.

Praised are You, Adonai our God, Sovereign of the Universe, who creates all kinds of spices.

Sniff the spices and pass the spice box around for everyone to sniff.

3. Now recite the blessing over the Havdalah candle:

בָּרוּךְ אַתָּה יְיָ אֱלֹהֵינוּ מֶלֶךְ הָעוֹלָם בּוֹרֵא מְאוֹרֵי הָאֵשׁ:

Baruch atah Adonai elohaynu melech ha'olam boray me'oray ha'aysh.

Praised are You, Adonai our God, Sovereign of the Universe, who creates the lights of the fire.

While the blessing is recited, family members hold out their hands with palms up, cup their hands, and look at the reflection of the flame on their fingernails.

4. Finally recite the final prayer:

בָּרוּךְ אַתָּה יְיָ אֱלֹהֵינוּ מֶלֶךְ הָעוֹלָם הַמַּבְדִּיל בֵּין קֹדֶשׁ לְחוֹל בֵּין אוֹר לְחֹשֶׁךְ בֵּין יִשְׂרָאֵל לָעַמִּים, בֵּין יוֹם הַשְּׁבִיעִי לְשֵׁשֶׁת יְמֵי הַמַּעֲשֶׂה: בָּרוּךְ אַתָּה יְיָ הַמַּבְדִּיל בֵּין קֹדֶשׁ לְחוֹל:

Baruch atah Adonai elohaynu melech ha'olam hamavdil bayn kodesh lechol bayn or lechoshech bayn Yisrael la'amim bayn yom hashevi'i le'sheshet yemay ha-ma'aseh. Baruch atah Adonai hamavdil bayn kodesh le-chol.

Praised are You, Adonai our God, Sovereign of the Universe, who makes a distinction between sacred and secular, light and darkness, Israel and other peoples, the seventh day and the six days of labor. Praised are You, Adonai, who makes a distinction between sacred and secular.

5. Many families conclude the service with the singing of Eliyahu ha-Navi ("Elijah the Prophet").

אֵלִיָּהוּ הַנָּבִיא, אֵלִיָּהוּ הַתִּשְׁבִּי
אֵלִיָּהוּ, אֵלִיָּהוּ, אֵלִיָּהוּ הַגִּלְעָדִי.
בִּמְהֵרָה בְיָמֵינוּ יָבֹא אֵלֵינוּ
עִם מָשִׁיחַ בֶּן דָּוִד.

Eliyahu ha-Navi Eliyahu ha-Tishbi
Eliyahu Eliyahu Eliyahu ha-Giladi.
Bimhera beyamaynu yavo aleynu
Im Mashiach ben David.

Elijah the Prophet
Elijah the Tishbite
Elijah the Gileadite.
May Elijah come quickly in our time
Along with the Messiah, the son of David.

6. Everyone takes a sip of the wine. Then pour some of שָׁבוּעַ טוֹב the remaining wine onto a plate (or directly over the flame) and put out the flame of the Havdalah candle. Shabbat is over, and everyone proclaims *shavua tov,* "a good week!" Often, people sing, *shavua tov, shavua tov, shavua tov, shavua tov,* "A good week, a week of peace. May gladness reign and joy increase."

Things to remember:

1. Havdalah is said about an hour after sunset on Saturday night, when three stars appear in the sky.

2. What you need:
   A Havdalah candle
   Cup of wine
   Spice box and spices

Key words and phrases:

Besamim בְּשָׂמִים. Spices.

Melaveh Malkah מְלַוֶּה מַלְכָּה. Meaning escorting the queen, it's a small meal or party held on Saturday evenings after Havdalah in some traditional Jewish communities.

Ner Havdalah נֵר הַבְדָּלָה. Twisted Havdalah candle.

If you want to know more:

Ron Isaacs. *Shabbat Delight: A Celebration in Stories, Songs and Games.* (Hoboken, 1987).

Ron Wolfson: *The Art of Jewish Living: The Shabbat Seder.* (Los Angeles, 1985).

Blowing a Shofar
תְּקִיעַת הַשׁוֹפָר

The source:

וְהַעֲבַרְתָּ שׁוֹפַר תְּרוּעָה בַּחֹדֶשׁ הַשְּׁבִעִי בֶּעָשׂוֹר לַחֹדֶשׁ בְּיוֹם הַכִּפּוּרִים תַּעֲבִירוּ שׁוֹפָר בְּכָל־אַרְצְכֶם:

"Then you shall sound the horn loud; in the seventh month, on the tenth day of the month—the Day of Atonement—you shall have the horn sounded throughout your land" (Lev. 25:9).

בַּחֹדֶשׁ הַשְּׁבִיעִי בְּאֶחָד לַחֹדֶשׁ יִהְיֶה לָכֶם שַׁבָּתוֹן זִכְרוֹן תְּרוּעָה מִקְרָא־קֹדֶשׁ:

"In the seventh month, on the first day of the month, you shall observe complete rest, a sacred occasion commemorated with loud blasts" (Lev. 23:24).

What you need to know:

A ram's horn is used because of its connection to the near sacrifice of Isaac which is read on the second day of Rosh Hashanah from Genesis 22. Prior to the beginning of the shofar service, the listener says the following blessing:

בָּרוּךְ אַתָּה יְיָ אֱלֹהֵנוּ מֶלֶךְ הָעוֹלָם אֲשֶׁר קִדְּשָׁנוּ בְּמִצְוֹתָיו וְצִוָּנוּ לִשְׁמוֹעַ קוֹל שׁוֹפָר:

Baruch atah Adonai elohaynu melech ha'olam asher kidshanu bemitzvotav vetzivanu lishmo'ah kol shofar.

Praised are You, Adonai our God, Sovereign of the Universe, who has made us holy with mitzvot and has instructed us to hear the call of the shofar.

בָּרוּךְ אַתָּה יְיָ אֱלֹהֵינוּ מֶלֶךְ הָעוֹלָם, שֶׁהֶחֱיָנוּ וְקִיְּמָנוּ וְהִגִּיעָנוּ לַזְּמַן הַזֶּה:

61

Baruch atah Adonai elohaynu melech ha'olam she-he-cheyanu ve-kimanu vehigiyanu lazman hazeh.

Praised are You, Adonai our God, Sovereign of the Universe, who has given us life, sustained us, and helped us reach this day.

Take out the shofar and blow the notes according to the order established by the caller.

תְּקִיעָה 1. *Tekiah:* lit. "blast," one long blast with a clean, consistent tone.

שְׁבָרִים 2. *Shevarim:* lit. "broken sound," three short calls together as long as *tekiah.*

תְּרוּעָה 3. *Teruah:* lit. "alarm," a rapid series of very short notes, generally three series of three that together total one *tekiah.*

תְּקִיעָה גְדוֹלָה 4. *Tekiah gedolah:* lit. "the great *tekiah,*" a single blast that is held as long as you can do it.

On Rosh Hashanah, after the Torah and Haftarah have been read, the shofar service begins. Specific verses from Psalms are read. Then the shofar blower makes two *berachot* (blessings).

Things to remember:

תְּקִיעָה
שְׁבָרִים
תְּרוּעָה
תְּקִיעָה
1. Beginning with the first day of the month of Elul (the month before Rosh Hashanah), it is a custom to blow the shofar. Some sound the entire *tekiah.* Do it every day (except Shabbat) except for the day before Rosh Hashanah.

2. Some keep the shofar concealed in the folds of the *tallit* until the caller (the one who calls the notes) is prepared to call the notes.

3. In shofar blowing, hearing and blowing so that other people can hear are considered equal *mitzvot.*

4. Each cycle has three repetitions. On the last, the *tekiah gedolah* is added.

Key words and phrases:

Akedat Yitzchak עֲקֵידַת יִצְחָק. The binding of Isaac.
Baal Tekiah בַּעַל תְּקִיעָה. Master blaster.
Seder tekiat shofar סֵדֶר תְּקִיעַת שׁוֹפָר. The order of the blowing of the shofar.

If you want to know more:

S. Y. Agnon, *Days of Awe* (New York, 1965).
Isaac Klein, *A Guide to Jewish Religious Practice* (New York, 1979).
Joel Grishaver, *Rosh Hashanah and Yom Kippur* (Los Angeles, 1987).

Tossing Tashlich
תַּשְׁלִיךְ

The source:

וְתַשְׁלִיךְ בִּמְצוּלוֹת יָם כָּל חַטֹּאתָם:

"You will cast all your sins into the depths of the sea" (Micah 7:19).

What you need to know:

1. On the afternoon of the first day of Rosh Hashanah, walk to a river or spring (preferably one with fish in it) and recite special prayers called penitential prayers. Here is the essence of them: Micah 7:18–20, Psalms 118:5–9; 33;130.

2. After you have said the prayers, empty your pockets (or throw bread crumbs which you have brought with you) into the water.

Things to remember:

1. Tossing the bread crumbs is symbolic of casting away our sins and starting over again in a new year.

2. If the first day of Rosh Hashanah falls on Shabbat, then *tashlich* is traditionally done on the second day.

Key words and phrases:

Avon עָוֹן. Intentional sin.
Chet חֵטְא. Missing the mark, mistaken sin.
Pesha פֶּשַׁע. The worst sin, done with malice.

If you want to know more:

Philip Goodman, *The Rosh Hashanah Anthology* (Philadelphia, 1970).

Building a Sukkah
סוּכָּה

The source:

בַּסֻּכֹּת תֵּשְׁבוּ שִׁבְעַת יָמִים

"You shall live in booths for seven days" (Lev. 23:42).

What you need to know:

1. A *sukkah* must have four walls. (One of the walls can be a wall of your own house.)

2. Start building the *sukkah* as soon after Yom Kippur as possible!

3. One possible *sukkah* building recipe is as follows:

   a. Use the back wall of your house or garage as one of the four walls.
   b. Stack two cement blocks in each corner and insert two-by-fours (seven or eight feet long) into the blocks. Connect the two-by-fours with one-by-twos across the middle and the top.
   c. Stretch burlap cloth or plastic, or nail some thin plywood over the frame. (Note: one wall can serve as the entrance if it is covered with burlap cloth.)
   d. Put one-by-ones running in both directions on the roof and cover with bamboo, twigs, corn husks, or other organic material. Remember to let the stars shine through!
   e. Decorate the inside of the *sukkah* with fruit hangings, Rosh Hashanah greeting cards, posters, paper chains, and the like.
   f. Hang an electric light fixture in the *sukkah* for dining in the evening. (Be careful!)
   g. If you do not want to build your *sukkah* from scratch there are prefabricated ones for sale at your local Judaica store or through your synagogue.

Sukkah diagram

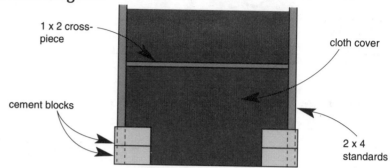

1 x 2 cross-piece

cloth cover

cement blocks

2 x 4 standards

SIDE VIEW OF END WALL

Key words and phrases:

Schach סְכַך. Organic material that is used to form the roof of a *sukkah*.

Ushpizin אוּשְׁפִּיזִין. Custom of inviting Jewish biblical ancestors into the *sukkah* as invisible guests.

If you want to know more:

Philip Goodman, *Sukkot and Simhat Torah Anthology* (Philadelphia, 1973).

The Four Species: Assembling the Lulav
אַרְבַּע מִינִים

The source:

וּלְקַחְתֶּם לָכֶם בַּיּוֹם הָרִאשׁוֹן פְּרִי עֵץ הָדָר כַּפֹּת תְּמָרִים וַעֲנַף עֵץ־עָבֹת וְעַרְבֵי־נָחַל וּשְׂמַחְתֶּם לִפְנֵי יְיָ אֱלֹהֵיכֶם שִׁבְעַת יָמִים:

"On the first day, you shall take the product of the beautiful trees, branches of palm trees, boughs of leafy trees, and willows of the brook, and you shall rejoice before Adonai your God for seven days" (Lev. 23:40).

What you need to know:

What to look for in the four species:

1. The four species consists of the *lulav* (palm), the *etrog* (citrus), the *hadas* (myrtle), and the *arava* (willow).

   לוּלָב
   אֶתְרוֹג
   הֲדַס
   עֲרָבָה

2. The *etrog* should taper upward on the top. Its face should be rough, and its shape symmetrical so that the tip is directly above the stem. There should be no blotches or spots on the skin and the color should be yellow.

3. The *lulav* should be fresh and straight. The leaves should not spread out nor should the tip be broken off. The minimum length is sixteen inches.

4. The myrtle and the willow should be green, fresh, with the leaves intact. The preferred length is approximately twelve inches.

To assemble the *lulav:*

1. Place the *lulav* in the Y-shaped holder.

2. Carefully place three myrtle leaves on the right and two willow twigs in the left part of the Y-shaped holder with the spine of the *lulav* facing you as the *lulav* is placed in the central part of the holder.

3. Take several leaves off of the *lulav* and tie them in a bow in three places along the length of the lulav.

Key words and phrases:

Arava עֲרָבָה. Willow leaves.
Etrog אֶתְרֹג. Citron.
Hadas הֲדַס. Myrtle leaves.
Lulav לוּלָב. Palm branch.
Okez עוֹקֵץ. The stem of the *etrog.*

Pittam פִּיטָם. The end of the *etrog* that produces the flower.

If you want to know more:

Encyclopaedia Judaica (Jerusalem, 1971) 6:1448–1449.
Morris Epstein, *All About Jewish Holidays and Customs* (New
    York, 1970).

More particulars:

1. After the festival of Sukkot is over, use the myrtle to
    make spices for your Havdalah spice box.

2. Use the *lulav* in the search—for—*chametz* ceremony (in-
    stead of a spoon). Then burn the *lulav* with your
    chametz at Passover, but be careful, dried *lulavim* can
    cut and pierce.

3. Stick a whole clove into your *etrog.* Cover it with pow-
    dered cinammon and let it dry for a few weeks. Then
    use it as a spice essence for Havdalah.

4. Or make *etrog* jelly with your used *etrog*!

Waving the Lulav
לוּלָב

The source:

וּלְקַחְתֶּם לָכֶם בַּיּוֹם הָרִאשׁוֹן פְּרִי עֵץ הָדָר כַּפֹּת תְּמָרִים וַעֲנַף עֵץ־עָבֹת וְעַרְבֵי־נָחַל וּשְׂמַחְתֶּם לִפְנֵי יְיָ אֱלֹהֵיכֶם שִׁבְעַת יָמִים:

"On the first day, you shall take the product of the beautiful trees, branches of palm trees, boughs of leafy trees, and willows of the brook, and you shall rejoice before Adonai your God for seven days" (Lev. 23:40).

What you need to know:

שַׁחֲרִית Wave the *lulav* each morning of Sukkot either before the
הַלֵּל   morning service (*Shacharit*) or during the service just
before *Hallel*.

Hold the entire *lulav* in your right hand (with the spine facing you, two willows on left, three myrtles on right), the *etrog* in the left. Both should touch each other. Before the blessing, hold the *etrog* with the *pittam* down. After the blessing (and during the waving), hold the *etrog* with the *pittam* up. Always stand facing east to Jerusalem.

After the meditation found in the *siddur* (prayerbook), recite this blessing:

בָּרוּךְ אַתָּה יְיָ אֱלֹהֵנוּ מֶלֶךְ הָעוֹלָם אֲשֶׁר קִדְּשָׁנוּ בְּמִצְוֹתָיו וְצִוָּנוּ עַל נְטִילַת לוּלָב:

Baruch atah Adonai elohaynu melech ha'olam asher kid-shanu bemitzvotav vetzivanu al netilat lulav.

Praised are You, Adonai our God, Sovereign of the Universe, who has made us holy by *mitzvot* and has instructed us to take hold of the *lulav*.

And on the first day:

בָּרוּךְ אַתָּה יְיָ אֱלֹהֵינוּ מֶלֶךְ הָעוֹלָם שֶׁהֶחֱיָנוּ וְקִיְּמָנוּ וְהִגִּיעָנוּ
לַזְּמַן הַזֶּה:

Baruch atah Adonai elohaynu melech ha'olam she-he-cheyanu vekimanu vehigiyanu lazman hazeh.

Praised are You, Adonai our God, Sovereign of the Universe, who has given us life, sustained us, and helped us to reach this day.

Shake the *lulav* in a motion of reaching out and reaching in, straightening your arms opposite your chest and folding them against your chest. Do this three times in front of you (east), then to the right (south), then back behind you over your shoulder (west), then out to the left (north), then above you (to heaven) and below you (to earth). Do it slowly and deliberately.

Also do it when these verses occur during *Hallel* (Psalms 113–118):

Hodu הוֹדוּ (front) *l'Adonai* לַיהֹוָה *kee* כִּי (right) *tov* טוֹב (back)
Kee כִּי (left) *l'olam* לְעֹלָם (up) *chasdo* חַסְדּוֹ (down)

Yomar יֹאמַר (front) *na* נָא (right) *Yisrael* יִשְׂרָאֵל (back)
Kee כִּי (left) *l'olam* לְעוֹלָם (up) *chasdo* חַסְדּוֹ (down)

Ana אָנָּא (front, right) *Adonai,* יְהֹוָה *hoshiah* הוֹשִׁיעָה (back, left, up) *na* נָא (down)
Ana אָנָּא (front, right) *Adonai,* יְהֹוָה, *hoshiah* הוֹשִׁיעָה (back, left, up) *na* נָא (down).

Things to remember:

1. Traditional Jews don't shake it on Shabbat.

2. Don't let the *pittam* get broken.

Key words and phrases:

Aravot עֲרָבוֹת. Willows.

Arba minim אַרְבַּע מִינִים. Four species (*etrog*/citron, palm, myrtle, willow).

Hadas הֲדַס. Leafy myrtle.

Hoshana הוֹשַׁע נָא. From the words *hoshiah na*, a fervent plea to God for help.

Lulav לוּלָב. Palm branch, used to name the combined branches because it is the largest.

Pittam פִּיטָם. Not the stem, the protrusion on the bottom of the *etrog*.

If you want to know more:

Encyclopaedia Judaica (Jerusalem, 1971) 15:495–502.

Philip Goodman, *The Sukkot and Simhat Torah Anthology* (Philadelphia, 1973).

Isaac Klein, *A Guide to Jewish Religious Practice* (New York, 1979).

Richard Siegel and Michael Strassfeld and Sharon Strassfeld, *The First Jewish Catalogue* (Philadelphia, 1973).

Lighting a Chanukiyah
הַדְלָקַת חֲנֻכִּיָּה

The source:

"The rabbis taught: The laws of Chanukah require one light for a person and household; those who want to be more careful may use one light for each member of the household. For those who want to be even more careful, the school of Shammai suggested that on the first day of the festival, eight candles are to be lit and we light one fewer each progressive night. Hillel suggested that on the first day, one candle is lit and one candle is added each night. Shammai reasoned that the number of candles corresponds to the number of days to come; Hillel reasoned that the number of candles corresponds to the days already passed" (Babylonian Talmud, Shabbat 21b).

What you need to know:

Place one new candle in the *chanukiyah* for each night of Chanukah, increasing one candle per night (plus the *shamash*). Olive oil may be used. Candles should be *placed* from right to left. Light the *shamash* first and use it to light from the *left*.

חֲנֻכִּיָּה
שַׁמָּשׁ

Then say the blessings:
(on each night)

בָּרוּךְ אַתָּה יְיָ אֱלֹהֵינוּ מֶלֶךְ הָעוֹלָם אֲשֶׁר קִדְּשָׁנוּ בְּמִצְוֹתָיו וְצִוָּנוּ לְהַדְלִיק נֵר שֶׁל חֲנֻכָּה:

Baruch atah Adonai elohaynu melech ha'olam asher kidshanu bemitzvotav vetzivanu lehadlik ner shel Chanukah.

Praised are You, Adonai our God, Sovereign of the Universe, who has made us holy by mitzvot and instructed us to light the Chanukah candles.

(on each night)

בָּרוּךְ אַתָּה יְיָ אֱלֹהֵינוּ מֶלֶךְ הָעוֹלָם שֶׁעָשָׂה נִסִּים לַאֲבוֹתֵינוּ בַּיָּמִים הָהֵם בַּזְּמַן הַזֶּה:

Baruch atah Adonai elohaynu melech ha'olam she'asah nisim lavotaynu bayamim hahaym bazman hazeh.

Praised are You, Adonai our God, Sovereign of the Universe, who performed miracles for our ancestors at this season in ancient days.

(on first night only)

בָּרוּךְ אַתָּה יְיָ אֱלֹהֵינוּ מֶלֶךְ הָעוֹלָם שֶׁהֶחֱיָנוּ וְקִיְּמָנוּ וְהִגִּיעָנוּ לַזְּמַן הַזֶּה:

Baruch atah Adonai elohaynu melech ha'olam she-he-cheyanu vekimanu vehigiyanu lazman hazeh.

Praised are You, Adonai our God, Sovereign of the Universe, who has given us life, sustained us, and helped us to reach this day.

Using the *shamash*, light the candles, one for each night, beginning with the current night first, from left to right. While some communities blow out the *shamash* each night and use it for the duration of the festival, most people let it burn down each night and use a new *shamash* for succeeding nights.

הַנֵּרוֹת הַלָּלוּ   After you have lit the candles, read the following prayer called *Hanerot Hallalu.*

הַנֵּרוֹת הַלָּלוּ אֲנַחְנוּ מַדְלִיקִין עַל הַנִּסִּים וְעַל הַנִּפְלָאוֹת וְעַל הַתְּשׁוּעוֹת וְעַל הַמִּלְחָמוֹת שֶׁעָשִׂיתָ לַאֲבוֹתֵינוּ בַּיָּמִים הָהֵם בַּזְּמַן הַזֶּה עַל יְדֵי כֹּהֲנֶיךָ הַקְּדוֹשִׁים. וְכָל־שְׁמוֹנַת יְמֵי חֲנֻכָּה הַנֵּרוֹת הַלָּלוּ קֹדֶשׁ הֵם, וְאֵין לָנוּ רְשׁוּת לְהִשְׁתַּמֵּשׁ בָּהֶם אֶלָּא לִרְאוֹתָם בִּלְבָד, כְּדֵי לְהוֹדוֹת וּלְהַלֵּל לְשִׁמְךָ הַגָּדוֹל, עַל נִסֶּיךָ וְעַל נִפְלְאוֹתֶיךָ וְעַל יְשׁוּעָתֶךָ:

In order to recall the miracles and wonders that You performed for our ancestors through the agency of

74

holy priests, we kindle these lights. We hold these flames sacred throughout the eight-day Chanukah period; we shall not make any profane use of them. Instead, we will simply look at them so that we may recall Your reputation as a God who makes miracles, does wonders, and delivers our people.

Things to remember:

1. Load from the right; light from the left.

2. Place your *chanukiyah* in the window nearest the street so that all can see.

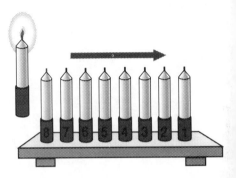

3. Candle holders in traditional *chanukiyot* are all on the same level, with a higher or separate *shamash*.

4. On Shabbat Chanukah, light the Chanukah candles before you light the Shabbat candles.

5. Light your candles after nightfall but early enough so that people can see them.

6. At the end of Shabbat Chanukah, do Havdalah and then light the Chanukah candles.

7. Don't use the lights of Chanukah for practical purposes, like reading.

Key words and phrases:

Ner נֵר. Candle.
Or אוֹר. Light.
Shemen שֶׁמֶן. Oil.

If you want to know more:

Elias Bickerman, *The Maccabees* (New York, 1947).
Encyclopaedia Judaica (Jerusalem, 1973) 7:1280–1315.

Philip Goodman, *The Hanukkah Anthology* (Philadelphia, 1976).

Mae Shafter Rockland, *The Hanukkah Book* (New York, 1975).

David Rosenberg, *A Blazing Fountain* (New York, 1978).

Sol Scharfstein, *Hanukah: Who? Why? When?* (Hoboken, N.J., 1991).

How to Play the Dreidel Game
דְרֵיידְל

The source:

Probably derived from an old German gambling game.

What you need to know:

1. Each person should start with ten or fifteen pennies, nuts, or raisins.

2. Each player puts a coin or raisin or nut into the middle (what card players call the pot).

3. Taking turns, one person spins at a time. Winning or losing is determined by which side of the dreidel is facing up when it falls.

4. a. *Nun* stands for "nothing" (*nisht* in Yiddish), so the נ player does nothing.
   b. *Gimmel* stands for "all" (*gantz* in Yiddish), so the ג player takes everything in the pot.
   c. *Heh* stands for "half," (*halb* in Yiddish), so the player ה takes half of what is in the pot.
   d. *Shin* stands for "put in" (*shtel* in Yiddish), so the ש player puts one in the pot.

5. After a *gimmel* has been spun, each player adds one. When an odd number of coins are in the pot, the player spinning *heh* takes half plus one. When one player has won everything, the game is over.

Things to remember:

1. Dreidels in Israel read *nes gadol hayah poh,* "a great miracle happened here" (instead of "there").

Key words and phrases:

Chanukah gelt. Coins used in dreidel game (often foil-wrapped chocolate).

Dreidel (Yiddish). Spinning top. *Sevivon* (Hebrew). Spinning top.

If you want to know more:

Philip Goodman, *The Hanukkah Anthology* (Philadelphia, 1976).

Sol Scharfstein, *Hanukah: Who? Why? When?* (Hoboken, N.J., 1991).

The Search for Chametz
בְּדִיקַת חָמֵץ

The source:

מַצּוֹת יֵאָכֵל אֵת שִׁבְעַת הַיָּמִים וְלֹא־יֵרָאֶה לְךָ חָמֵץ וְלֹא־יֵרָאֶה
לְךָ שְׂאֹר בְּכָל־גְּבֻלֶךָ:

"Unleavened bread shall be eaten throughout the seven days; and there shall be no leavened bread or leavening seen with you, in all of your borders" (Exod. 13:7).

What you need to know:

1. The search for *chametz* begins on the evening following the thirteenth of Nisan. (If the first day of Passover is on Sunday, then the search is conducted on the evening following the twelfth of Nisan.)

2. To conduct the search for *chametz*, you will need a candle, a feather, and a wooden spoon.

3. To make sure that the search for *chametz* is successful, several pieces of bread are scattered throughout various parts of the house to be collected during the search.

4. Before the actual search begins, light a candle and recite this blessing:

בָּרוּךְ אַתָּה יְיָ אֱלֹהֵנוּ מֶלֶךְ הָעוֹלָם אֲשֶׁר קִדְּשָׁנוּ בְּמִצְוֹתָיו וְצִוָּנוּ
עַל בְּעוּר־חָמֵץ:

Baruch atah Adonai elohaynu melech ha'olam asher kidshanu bemitzvotav vetzivanu al bi'ur chametz.

Praised are You, Adonai our God, Sovereign of the Universe, who has made us holy with mitzvot and instructed us to remove the leaven.

5. The search begins. When a piece of bread is discovered, sweep it onto the wooden spoon using the feather. Then place it into a bag for disposal.

6. After all of the pieces of bread have been gathered and placed into the bag, say the following:

כָּל־חֲמִירָא וַחֲמִיעָא, דְּאִכָּא בִרְשׁוּתִי, דְּלָא חֲמִיתֵּהּ וּדְלָא בְעַרְתֵּהּ, וּדְלָא יָדַעְנָא לֵהּ, לִבְטֵל וְלֶהֱוֵי הֶפְקֵר, כְּעַפְרָא דְאַרְעָא:

Kol chamira vechamiya de'ikah virshuti dela chamitay u'dela vay'artei udela yadana lay libtayl ve'lehevay hefker ke'afra de'ara.

Any leaven that may still be in the house, which I have not seen or have not removed, shall be as if it does not exist, and as the dust of the earth.

7. The next day (on the fourteenth of Nisan), at about ten o'clock in the morning, take all the leaven still remaining in the house together with the leaven collected during the search the previous night and burn it. When the leaven is burned, again recite the following:

כָּל־חֲמִירָא וַחֲמִיעָא, דְּאִכָּא בִּרְשׁוּתִי, דַּחֲמִיתֵּהּ וּדְלָא חֲמִיתֵּהּ, דְּבַעַרְתֵּהּ וּדְלָא בַעַרְתֵּהּ, לִבְטֵל וְלֶהֱוֵי הֶפְקֵר, כְּעַפְרָא דְאַרְעָא:

Kol chamira vachamiya de'ika birshuti (dechamitay) u'dela chamitay devayartay u'dela vayartay libtayl ve'lehavay hefker ke'afra de'ara.

Any leaven that may still be in the house (which I have seen and not seen, which I have or have not removed,) shall be as if it does not exist, and as the dust of the earth.

Things to remember:

1. Leaven (*chametz* in Hebrew) is fermented dough made from the flour of wheat, rye, barley, spelt, or oats. According to Jewish law, eating *chametz* or even having it in your possession is forbidden during the festival of Passover.

2. Before Passover begins, all traces of leaven must be removed from the house. All utensils and cookware must also be free from *chametz.*

3. Some people use the *lulav* from the preceding Sukkot as fuel to burn the *chametz.*

4. Leaven in rabbinic literature has often symbolized the evil impulse in a person. When you remove the leaven from your home prior to Passover, you are also symbolically removing evilness from your heart.

Key words and phrases:

Biur chametz בְּעוּר חָמֵץ. Burning the leaven.
Chametz חָמֵץ. Leaven.

If you want to know more:

Philip Goodman, *The Passover Anthology* (Philadelphia, 1962).
Morris Epstein, *All About Jewish Holidays and Customs* (New York, 1970).
Ron Wolfson, *The Art of Jewish Living* (New York, 1988).

Making Matzah
מַצָּה

The source:

בָּרִאשֹׁן בְּאַרְבָּעָה עָשָׂר יוֹם לַחֹדֶשׁ בָּעֶרֶב תֹּאכְלוּ מַצֹּת עַד יוֹם הָאֶחָד וְעֶשְׂרִים לַחֹדֶשׁ בָּעָרֶב:

"In the first month, on the fourteenth day of the month in the evening, you shall eat unleavened bread, until the twenty-first of the month in the evening" (Exod. 12:18).

What you need to know:

1. Mix Passover flour and water and knead to make the dough.

2. Using a rolling pin, roll the dough into a flat sheet.

3. Perforate the dough to remove all air bubbles.

4. Bake in oven at 500° for no more than eighteen minutes.

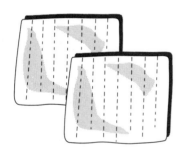

Things to remember:

1. For flour to be Passover flour, it has to be supervised as soon as the wheat is milled.

Key words and phrases:

Egg matzah. Matzah that is enriched and more easily digested, eaten only by very young children and people who have specific health needs.
Derlanger. Person putting matzah dough onto rolling pin.
Matzah brei. An omelette made with eggs and matzah that is fried in a pan.
Matzah shemurah. Hand–made matzah.

Mehl mester. Person who measures amount of flour required by the matzah kneader.

Redel. Sharp-toothed wheel used to make perforations in matzah dough.

Redler. Person who makes the matzah perforations.

Shiber. Person responsible for placing matzah dough into oven.

Treger. Person who carries finished matzah to the plate where it was to be packed.

Uggot matzah. Matzah that is round in shape.

Vasser-gisser. Person that pours cold water into the dough as the matzah kneader requires.

If you want to know more:

Encyclopaedia Judaica (Jerusalem, 1973) 11:1155.

Philip Goodman, *The Passover Anthology* (Philadelphia, 1961).

More particulars:

1. Matzah was first baked to serve unexpected visitors. When the angels visited Lot in Sodom, Lot offered them hospitality and baked unleavened bread for them (Gen. 19:3).

2. In Talmudic times some *matzot* were made with designs on them, including figures of fish and doves.

3. In the Middle Ages *matzot* were made one inch thick!

4. Until the nineteenth century *matzot* were usually round in shape.

5. Until the middle of the nineteenth century all *matzot* were baked by hand.

6. In 1857 the first matzah-baking machine was invented in Austria.

7. In the middle of the nineteenth century the growth of Jewish communities was often measured by the amount of matzah that community consumed.

Setting the Seder Table
שֻׁלְחַן הַסֵּדֶר

The source:

Mishnah and Talmud, tractate Pesachim.

What you need to know:

1. Make sure you have a Haggadah for each person.

2. Your Seder plate should look like this:

Make sure you remember to include a hard-boiled egg, a roasted lamb bone (chicken neck), greens, bitter herbs, salt water, and *charoset*.

3. Provide salt water for dipping for everyone.

4. Cut up enough greens—parsley or celery—for all.

5. You can use horseradish or romaine lettuce as a bitter herb, but make sure you have enough for everyone.

6. Be sure to include *charoset*. (There are lots of different recipes depending on the community.) It usually contains apples, nuts, cinnamon, and a little wine.

7. Place three *matzot* on a plate or in a three–layer *matzot* cover if you have one.

8. Provide enough wine–four cups for each person.

9. Place a pillow on each chair for reclining.

10. Don't forget a cup for Elijah and holiday candles. Flowers are nice too.

11. You will want to provide a cup, basin, and towel for washing, as well.

Things to remember:

1. Try to have matching *Haggadot* for everyone at the table.

2. If you have a large gathering for the Seder, you may want to set two Seder plates, one at each end of the table.

Key words and phrases:

Haggadah הַגָּדָה. Story/prayerbook for the Passover Seder.

If you want to know more:

Philip Goodman, *The Passover Anthology* (Philadelphia, 1961).
Kerry Olitzky and Ron Isaacs, *The Discovery Haggadah* (Hoboken, N.J., 1992).

Leading the Seder
סֵדֶר

The sources:

Exodus 12:3–11, 26–11, 26–27; Exodus 13:8, 13:14; Deuteronomy 6:20–21.

What you need to know:

The Order of the Seder

קַדֵּשׁ 1. *Kadesh:* Kiddush (sanctification) over the first cup (of four) of wine. Drink it in a comfortable position.

וּרְחַץ 2. *Urchatz:* Wash your hands—but without the usual blessing. It is an old custom to wash before dipping foods in a liquid or sauce.

כַּרְפַּס 3. *Karpas:* Eat the greens dipped in salt water. Green symbolizes spring; salt water reminds us of the salty tears of our ancestors who endured slavery.

יַחַץ 4. *Yachatz:* Break the middle of the matzah. Half of it is for the afikoman.

מַגִּיד 5. *Maggid:* Tell the story of Passover. This is really what the Haggadah is all about. It includes the Four Questions, the Four Sons (and we add daughters), and the Ten Plagues. This section ends with the second cup of wine. Make sure you drink it in a comfortable position.

רָחְצָה 6. *Rachtzah:* With the proper blessing, wash your hands before you begin the meal.

מוֹצִיא מַצָּה 7–8. *Motzi-Matzah:* This is a double blessing said over the matzah (as unleavened bread and as a bread substitute) just prior to eating the meal. Eat the matzah (the top and half of the middle of the three) in a comfortable position.

9. *Maror:* After saying the appropriate blessing, eat the horseradish.　מָרוֹר

10. *Korech:* Called the Hillel sandwich; eat a sandwich made of matzah, horseradish, and *charoset.* Use the bottom matzah.　כּוֹרֵךְ

11. *Shulchan Orech:* Now is the time to eat all those good things on the table. Don't forget to keep on singing!　שׁוּלְחָן עוֹרֵךְ

12. *Tzafun:* Dessert time—but begin with eating the hidden *afikoman* (once it is found or ransomed).　צָפוּן

13. *Barech: Birkat Hamazon,* grace after the meal. Say it over the third cup of wine while you are in a comfortable position.　בָּרֵךְ

14. *Hallel:* Say the *Hallel* psalms. After you are finished, drink the fourth cup of wine. Don't forget to stay comfortable. Then pour Elijah's cup and have someone open the door for him.　הַלֵּל

15. *Nirtzah:* This concludes the meal.　נִרְצָה

Remember to say, "Next year in Jerusalem." Beginning with the second night of Passover, count the *Omer.*

Things to remember:

1. Give participants a chance to participate.

2. Don't just rely on the Haggadah text. Encourage discussion and questioning.

Key words and phrases:

Maimuna. A feast held by Moroccan Jews the day after Passover to make the holiday last longer.

If you want to know more:

Nahum N. Glatzer, *The Passover Haggadah* (New York, 1967).

Kerry Olitzky and Ronald Isaacs, *The Discovery Haggadah* (Hoboken, N.J., 1992).

Haim Raphael, *A Feast of History* (New York, 1972).

Counting the Omer
סְפִירַת הָעוֹמֶר

The source:

וּסְפַרְתֶּם לָכֶם מִמָּחֳרַת הַשַּׁבָּת מִיּוֹם הֲבִיאֲכֶם אֶת־עֹמֶר הַתְּ־
נוּפָה שֶׁבַע שַׁבָּתוֹת תְּמִימֹת תִּהְיֶינָה׃

"And from the day on which you bring the sheaf of wave offering—the day after the Sabbath(–first day of Passover)—you shall count off seven weeks. They must be complete" (Lev. 23:15).

What you need to know:

1. Beginning with the second night of Pesach, and ending with Shavuot, recite the following meditation and *kavanah* (available in most complete prayerbooks).

הִנְנִי מְקַיֵּם מִצְוַת עֲשֵׂה שֶׁל סְפִירַת הָעֹמֶר כְּמוֹ שֶׁכָּתוּב בַּתּוֹרָה.
וּסְפַרְתֶּם לָכֶם מִמָּחֳרַת הַשַּׁבָּת מִיּוֹם הֲבִיאֲכֶם אֶת־עֹמֶר הַתְּ־
נוּפָה שֶׁבַע שַׁבָּתוֹת תְּמִימֹת תִּהְיֶינָה עַד מִמָּחֳרַת הַשַּׁבָּת
הַשְּׁבִיעִית תִּסְפְּרוּ חֲמִשִּׁים יוֹם׃

I am now prepared to fulfill the positive mitzvah of counting the *omer* just as it is written in the Torah. And from the day on which you bring the sheaf of wave offering—the day after the day of rest—you shall count off seven weeks. They must be complete. Until the day after the seventh week you should count fifty days.

2. Recite the following blessing:

בָּרוּךְ אַתָּה יְיָ אֱלֹהֵנוּ מֶלֶךְ הָעוֹלָם אֲשֶׁר קִדְּשָׁנוּ בְּמִצְוֹתָיו וְצִוָּנוּ
עַל סְפִירַת הָעֹמֶר׃

Baruch atah Adonai elohaynu melech ha'olam asher kidshanu bemitzvotav vetzivanu al s'firat ha-omer.

Praised are You, Adonai our God, Sovereign of the Universe, who makes us holy with mitzvot and instructed us to count the *omer*.

3. Using the following formula, count each day. Today is the ___ day, which is ___ weeks and ___ in the *omer*.

הַיּוֹם ___ יוֹם שֶׁהֵם ___ שָׁבוּעוֹת וְ___ יָמִים לָעוֹמֶר

4. Then read the following Psalm (57) and the prayer following:

We beseech You to release Your captive nation by the mighty strength of Your right hand. Accept the joyous chant of Your people. Lift us and purify us, O revered God. O mighty One, guard them that meditate on Your unity. Bless them. Purify them. Have mercy on them. Bestow Your charity on them. O peaceful and holy Being, in Your abundant goodness, lead Your congregation. You who are the only and exalted God, turn to Your people who are mindful of Your holiness. Accept our prayer and hearken to our cry, for You know all secrets. Praised be Your name, whose great Sovereignty is forever and ever.

5. And now, this prayer:

Master of the Universe, through Moses Your servant You have instructed us to count the days of the *omer* in order to help us keep ourselves free from enveloping uncleanness. Therefore, You ordained in Your Torah: "From the morrow after the day of rest, from the day of your bringing the sheaf (*omer*) of the wave-offering you shall count for yourselves seven weeks; complete they shall be, until the fiftieth day," so that Your people Israel might keep themselves free from contamination. Therefore may it be Your will, Adonai our God and God of our ancestors, that the counting of the *omer* which I have done this day may help complete my counting until now, and make me feel clean and made holy through Your divine holiness. May its influence be felt in all spheres of life. May it strengthen my soul and my spirit against all corruption, helping purify me, and inspire me through Your supreme sanctity. Amen. Selah.

Things to remember:

1. *Omer* links the Exodus with the giving of Torah. We count the days of our freedom in anticipation of our people's encounter with God.

2. In Psalm 67:5, the line has forty-nine letters, one for each day.

3. Do the counting while standing, in the evening after three stars come out. Some people also say it in the morning (without the blessing).

4. Since the period of the counting is a semi-mourning period, weddings and certain other events don't take place, except on the 33rd day—Lag Ba-Omer (Iyar 18). There are actually two primary customs for this mourning period. One is from Passover until Lag Ba-Omer; the other is from Rosh Chodesh Iyar until three days before Shavuot.

5. In this context, Sabbath, the day of rest, refers to the first day of Pesach.

Key words and phrases:

Sefirat Ha-omer סְפִירַת הָעֹמֶר. Counting of the *omer*.
Omer עוֹמֶר. Grain measurement.
Wave offering. Barley, the first to ripen of the grains sown in winter, it was solemnly cut in the field and brought to the Temple in thanksgiving.

If you want to know more:

Michael Strassfield, *The Jewish Holidays* (New York, 1985).
Isaac Klein, *A Guide to Jewish Religious Practice* (New York, 1979).
Arthur Waskow, *Seasons of Our Joy* (New York, 1982).

Leading Birkat Hamazon
בִּרְכַּת הַמָּזוֹן

The source:

וְאָכַלְתָּ וְשָׂבָעְתָּ וּבֵרַכְתָּ אֶת־יְיָ אֱלֹהֶיךָ עַל־הָאָרֶץ הַטֹּבָה אֲשֶׁר נָתַן־לָךְ:

"When you have eaten your fill, give thanks to God for the good land which God has given you" (Deut. 8:10).

What you need to know:

בִּרְכַּת הַמָּזוֹן
הַמּוֹצִיא

1. *Birkat Hamazon* (grace/blessing after the meal) is recited after any meal which began with the blessing over bread (*hamotzi*).

מְזוּמָן
רַבּוֹתַי נְבָרֵךְ

2. When at least three people eat together, they constitute a *mezuman*. One of the three is asked to call the others to say *Birkat Hamazon* through an introductory formula which begins, *Rabbotai nevarech* ("let us say grace").

3. It is the custom to give the honor of leading *Birkat Hamazon* to a guest.

4. Before *Birkat Hamazon*, some have the custom of removing all utensils (especially knives) from the table, and leaving a piece of bread (or crumbs) on the table. Knives were used as weapons of war, and the table is considered an altar of peace and tranquility.

בְּרָכָה
אַחֲרוֹנָה

5. After eating food consisting of cake, wine, and so forth (without bread), there is a special blessing called a *beracha acharona* which is recited. This is a sort of abridged version of *Birkat Hamazon*.

When three or more adults have eaten together, one of them formally invites the others to join in these blessings. (When ten or more are present add the words in parentheses.)

רַבּוֹתַי נְבָרֵךְ:

Rabotai nevaraych

Friends, let us give thanks.

The others respond, and the leader repeats:

יְהִי שֵׁם יְיָ מְבֹרָךְ מֵעַתָּה וְעַד עוֹלָם:

Yehi shem Adonai mevorach may'atah ve'ad olam.

May God be praised now and forever.

The leader continues:

בִּרְשׁוּת רַבּוֹתַי, נְבָרֵךְ (אֱלֹהֵינוּ) שֶׁאָכַלְנוּ מִשֶּׁלּוֹ:

Bireshut rabotai, nevaraych (elohaynu) she'achalnu mishelo.

With your consent, friends, let us praise (our God) the One of whose food we have partaken.

The others respond, and the leader repeats:

בָּרוּךְ (אֱלֹהֵינוּ) שֶׁאָכַלְנוּ מִשֶּׁלּוֹ וּבְטוּבוֹ חָיִינוּ:

Baruch (elohaynu) she'achalnu mishelo uvetuvo cha'yinu.

Praised be (our God) the One whose food we have partaken and by whose goodness we live.

Leaders and others:

בָּרוּךְ הוּא וּבָרוּךְ שְׁמוֹ:

Baruch hu uvaruch shemo.

Praised be God and praised be God's name.

בָּרוּךְ אַתָּה יְיָ אֱלֹהֵינוּ מֶלֶךְ הָעוֹלָם, הַזָּן אֶת הָעוֹלָם כֻּלּוֹ בְּטוּבוֹ, בְּחֵן, בְּחֶסֶד וּבְרַחֲמִים. הוּא נוֹתֵן לֶחֶם לְכָל־בָּשָׂר כִּי לְעוֹלָם חַסְדּוֹ. וּבְטוּבוֹ הַגָּדוֹל תָּמִיד לֹא חָסַר לָנוּ וְאַל יֶחְסַר לָנוּ מָזוֹן לְעוֹלָם וָעֶד בַּעֲבוּר שְׁמוֹ הַגָּדוֹל, כִּי הוּא אֵל זָן וּמְפַרְנֵס לַכֹּל וּמֵטִיב לַכֹּל וּמֵכִין מָזוֹן לְכָל־בְּרִיּוֹתָיו אֲשֶׁר בָּרָא: בָּרוּךְ אַתָּה יְיָ, הַזָּן אֶת־הַכֹּל:

Baruch atah Adonai, elohaynu melech ha'olam, hazan et ha'olam kulo betuvo, bechayn, bechesed, uverachamim. Hu notayn lechem lechol basar, ki le'olam chasdo. Uvetuvo hagadol, tamid lo chasar lanu, ve'al yechsar lanu mazon le'olam va'ed ba'avur shemo hagadol, ki hu El zan umefarnays lakol, umaytiv lakol, umaychin mazon lechol beriyotav asher bara. Baruch atah Adonai, hazan et hakol.

Praised are You, our God, Sovereign of the Universe, who sustains the whole word with kindness and compassion. God provides food for every creature, for God's love endures forever. God's great goodness has never failed us. God's great glory assures us nourishment. All life is God's creation and God's good to all, providing every creature with food and sustenance. Praised are You, God, who sustains all life.

נוֹדֶה לְךָ יְיָ אֱלֹהֵינוּ עַל שֶׁהִנְחַלְתָּ לַאֲבוֹתֵינוּ אֶרֶץ חֶמְדָּה טוֹבָה וּרְחָבָה, בְּרִית וְתוֹרָה, חַיִּים וּמָזוֹן. יִתְבָּרַךְ שִׁמְךָ בְּפִי כָּל־חַי תָּמִיד לְעוֹלָם וָעֶד, כַּכָּתוּב וְאָכַלְתָּ וְשָׂבָעְתָּ וּבֵרַכְתָּ אֶת־יְיָ אֱלֹהֶיךָ עַל־הָאָרֶץ הַטּוֹבָה אֲשֶׁר נָתַן לָךְ. בָּרוּךְ אַתָּה יְיָ, עַל הָאָרֶץ וְעַל הַמָּזוֹן:

Nodeh lecha Adonai elohaynu al shehinchalta la'avotaynu eretz chemdah, tovah urechavah, brit vetorah, cha'yim umazon. Yitbarach shimcha befi kol chai tamid le'olam va'ed. Kakatuv ve'achalta vesavata uvayrachta et Adonai Elohecha al ha'aretz hatovah asher natan lach. Baruch atah Adonai, al ha'aretz ve'al hamazon.

We thank you, God, for the pleasing, ample, desirable land which You gave to our ancestors, for the covenant and Torah, for life and sustenance. May You forever be praised by all who live, as it is written in the Torah: "When you have eaten and are satisfied, you shall praise God for the good land which God has given you." Praised are You, God, for the land and for sustenance.

וּבְנֵה יְרוּשָׁלַיִם עִיר הַקֹּדֶשׁ בִּמְהֵרָה בְיָמֵינוּ. בָּרוּךְ אַתָּה יְיָ בּוֹנֵה בְרַחֲמָיו יְרוּשָׁלָיִם. אָמֵן:

Uvenay Yerushala'yim ir hakodesh bimhayrah ve'ya-maynu. Baruch atah Adonai, boneh verachamav Yerusha-la'yim. Amen.

Fully rebuild Jerusalem, the holy city, soon, in our time. Praised are You, God, who in mercy rebuilds Jerusalem. Amen.

בָּרוּךְ אַתָּה יְיָ אֱלֹהֵינוּ מֶלֶךְ הָעוֹלָם, הַמֶּלֶךְ הַטּוֹב וְהַמֵּטִיב לַכֹּל. הוּא הֵטִיב הוּא מֵטִיב, הוּא יֵיטִיב לָנוּ, הוּא גְמָלָנוּ, הוּא גוֹמְלֵנוּ, הוּא יִגְמְלֵנוּ לָעַד חֵן וָחֶסֶד וְרַחֲמִים וִיזַכֵּנוּ לִימוֹת הַמָּשִׁיחַ:

Barukh atah Adonai, elohaynu melech ha'olam, hamelech hatov vehamaytiv lakol. Hu haytiv, hu maytiv, hu yay-tiv lanu. Hu gemalanu, hu gomlaynu, hu yigmileynu la'ad chayn vechesed verachamim, viyzakaynu liymot hamashiach.

Praised are You, God, Sovereign of the Universe, who are good to all, whose goodness is constant through all time. Favor us with kindness and compassion now and in the future as in the past. May we be worthy of the days of the Messiah.

הָרַחֲמָן, הוּא יַנְחִילֵנוּ יוֹם שֶׁכֻּלוֹ שַׁבָּת וּמְנוּחָה לְחַיֵּי הָעוֹלָמִים:

Harachaman hu yanchilaynu yom shekulo Shabbat umenucha lecha'yay ha'olamim.

May the Merciful grant us a day of true Shabbat rest, reflecting the life of eternity.

וְנִשָּׂא בְרָכָה מֵאֵת יְיָ וּצְדָקָה מֵאֱלֹהֵי יִשְׁעֵנוּ, וְנִמְצָא חֵן וְשֵׂכֶל טוֹב בְּעֵינֵי אֱלֹהִים וְאָדָם. עֹשֶׂה שָׁלוֹם בִּמְרוֹמָיו, הוּא יַעֲשֶׂה שָׁלוֹם, עָלֵינוּ וְעַל כָּל יִשְׂרָאֵל, וְאִמְרוּ אָמֵן:

Venisa verachah may'ayt Adonai utzedakah may'elohay yishaynu. Venimtza chayn vesaychel tov be'aynay elohim ve'adam. Oseh shalom bimromav hu ya'aseh shalom alaynu ve'al kol Yisra'el. Ve'imru Amen.

May we receive blessings from God, loving–kindness from the God of our deliverance. May we find grace and good favor before God and all people. May God who brings peace to the universe bring peace to us and to all the people Israel. And let us say: Amen.

Key words and phrases:

Hamezamen הַמְזַמֵּן. The leader who leads *Birkat Hamazon*.
Mezuman מְזוּמָן. Unit consisting of a minimum of three adult Jews which as a group recites *Birkat Hamazon* aloud.

If you want to know more:

Hayim Donin, *To Pray as a Jew* (New York, 1980).
Isaac Klein, *A Guide to Jewish Religious Practice* (New York, 1979).
Joel Grishaver, *Basic Berachot* (Los Angeles, 1988).

Lighting the Memorial Candle
נֵר זִכָּרוֹן

The source:

נֵר יְהֹוָה נִשְׁמַת אָדָם

Many sources for this custom have been suggested including Proverbs 20:27, "The soul of the human being is the lamp of Adonai."

What you need to know:

1. While there are no specific rituals for lighting a memorial candle, the lighting should take place in a sacred context. Therefore, we recommend that you say the following before lighting the candle. If you prefer, as an alternative, simply speak from the heart.
    O God, grant us strength as we mourn the loss of ___. We will always have cherished memories of him/her. Bless our family with light and peace. May ___'s memory continue to serve as a blessing and an inspiration to all who knew and loved him/her.

2. Light the candle.

3. Then say the following:

זִכְרוֹנוֹ (זִכְרוֹנָה) לִבְרָכָה

Zichrono (Zichrona) liveracha. His (her) memory is a blessing.

4. *Kaddish* and/or *El Malei Rachamim* (a prayer for resting souls) is also often recited at this time.

יִתְגַּדַּל וְיִתְקַדַּשׁ שְׁמֵהּ רַבָּא בְּעָלְמָא דִי בְרָא כִרְעוּתֵהּ וְיַמְלִיךְ מַלְכוּתֵהּ בְּחַיֵּיכוֹן וּבְיוֹמֵיכוֹן וּבְחַיֵּי דְכָל בֵּית יִשְׂרָאֵל, בַּעֲגָלָא וּבִזְמַן קָרִיב וְאִמְרוּ אָמֵן: יְהֵא שְׁמֵהּ רַבָּא מְבָרַךְ לְעָלַם וּלְעָלְמֵי עָלְמַיָּא: יִתְבָּרַךְ וְיִשְׁתַּבַּח וְיִתְפָּאַר וְיִתְרוֹמַם וְיִתְנַשֵּׂא וְיִתְהַדָּר וְיִתְעַלֶּה וְיִתְהַלָּל שְׁמֵהּ דְּקוּדְשָׁא, בְּרִיךְ הוּא לְעֵלָּא (בעשי״ת וּלְעֵלָּא מִכָּל) מִן כָּל בִּרְכָתָא וְשִׁירָתָא, תֻּשְׁבְּחָתָא וְנֶחֱמָתָא, דַּאֲמִירָן בְּעָלְמָא, וְאִמְרוּ אָמֵן: יְהֵא שְׁלָמָא רַבָּא מִן שְׁמַיָּא וְחַיִּים עָלֵינוּ וְעַל כָּל יִשְׂרָאֵל וְאִמְרוּ אָמֵן: עוֹשֶׂה שָׁלוֹם בִּמְרוֹמָיו הוּא יַעֲשֶׂה שָׁלוֹם עָלֵינוּ וְעַל כָּל יִשְׂרָאֵל וְאִמְרוּ אָמֵן:

Yit-ga-dal ve-yit-ka-dash she-mei ra-ba be-al-ma di-ve-ra chi-re-u-tei, ve-yam-lich mal-chutei be-cha-yei-chon u-ve-yo-mei-chon u-ve-cha-yei de-chol beit Yis-ra-el, ba-a-ga-la u-vi-ze-man ka-riv, ve-i-me-ru: a-mein. Ye-hei she-mei ra-ba me-va-rach le-a-lam u-le-al-mei al-ma-ya. Yit-ba-rach ve-yish-ta-bach, ve-yit-pa-ar ve-yit-ro-mam ve-yit-na-sei, ve-yit-ha-dar ve-yit-a-leh ve-yit-ha-lal she-mei de-ku-de-sha, be-rich hu, le-ei-la min kol bi-re-cha-ta ve-shi-ra-ta, tush-becha-ta ve-ne-che-ma-ta, da-a mi-ran be-al-ma, ve-i-me-ru; a-mein. Ye-hei she-la-ma ra-ba min she-ma-ya ve-cha-yim a-lei-nu ve-al kol Yis-ra-eil, ve-i-me-ru: a-mein. O-seh sha-lom bi-me-ro-mav, hu ya-a-seh sha-lom a-lei-nu ve-al kol Yis-ra-eil, ve-i-me-ru: a-mein.

Let the glory of God be extolled, let God's great name be hallowed, in the world whose creation God willed. May God's sovereignty soon prevail, in our own day, our own lives, and the life of all Israel, and let us say Amen. Let God's great name be blessed for ever and ever. Let the name of God be glorified, exalted, and honored, though God is beyond all the praises, songs, and adorations that we can utter, and let us say Amen. For us and for all Israel, may the blessing of peace and the promise of life come true, and let us say Amen. May God who causes peace to reign in the high heavens, let peace descend on us, on all Israel and all the world, and let us say: Amen.

אֵל מָלֵא רַחֲמִים
Eil Malei Rachamim

For male

אֵל מָלֵא רַחֲמִים, שׁוֹכֵן בַּמְּרוֹמִים, הַמְצֵא מְנוּחָה נְכוֹנָה תַּחַת כַּנְפֵי הַשְּׁכִינָה, בְּמַעֲלוֹת קְדוֹשִׁים וּטְהוֹרִים כְּזֹהַר הָרָקִיעַ מַזְהִירִים, אֶת־נִשְׁמַת ___ בֶּן ___ שֶׁהָלַךְ לְעוֹלָמוֹ, בְּגַן עֵדֶן תְּהֵא מְנוּחָתוֹ. אָנָּא, בַּעַל הָרַחֲמִים הַסְתִּירֵהוּ בְּסֵתֶר כְּנָפֶיךָ לְעוֹלָמִים, וּצְרוֹר בִּצְרוֹר הַחַיִּים אֶת־נִשְׁמָתוֹ, יְיָ הוּא נַחֲלָתוֹ, וְיָנוּחַ בְּשָׁלוֹם עַל מִשְׁכָּבוֹ, וְנֹאמַר אָמֵן:

Eil malei rachamim sho-chein bam'romim, ham-tzei m'nuchah n'chonah tachat kanfei ha-sh'chinah, b'ma-alot k'doshim u-t'horim k'zohar ha-rakiya maz-hirim et nish-mat ____ ben ___ she-halach l'olamo, b'gan eiden t'hei menuchato. Ana, ba-al ha-rachamim, hastireihu b'seiter k'nafecha l'olamim, u-tzror bi-tzror ha-chayim et nishmato, Adonai hu nachalato, v'yanu'ach b'shalom al mishkavo, v'nomar amen.

God of compassion, grant perfect peace in Your sheltering Presence, among the holy and the pure who shine in the brightness of the firmament, to the soul of our dear ___ who has gone to his eternal rest. God of compassion, remember all his worthy deeds in the land of the living. May his soul be bound up in the bond of everlasting life. May God be his inheritance. May he rest in peace. And let us answer: Amen.

For female

אֵל מָלֵא רַחֲמִים, שׁוֹכֵן בַּמְּרוֹמִים, הַמְצֵא מְנוּחָה נְכוֹנָה תַּחַת כַּנְפֵי הַשְּׁכִינָה, בְּמַעֲלוֹת קְדוֹשִׁים וּטְהוֹרִים כְּזֹהַר הָרָקִיעַ מַזְהִירִים, אֶת־נִשְׁמַת ___ בַּת ___ שֶׁהָלְכָה לְעוֹלָמָה, בְּגַן עֵדֶן תְּהֵא מְנוּחָתָה. אָנָּא, בַּעַל הָרַחֲמִים הַסְתִּירֶהָ בְּסֵתֶר כְּנָפֶיךָ לְעוֹלָמִים, וּצְרוֹר בִּצְרוֹר הַחַיִּים אֶת־נִשְׁמָתָה, יְיָ הוּא נַחֲלָתָה, וְתָנוּחַ בְּשָׁלוֹם עַל מִשְׁכָּבָה, וְנֹאמַר אָמֵן:

Eil malei rachamim sho-chein bam'romim, ham-tzei m'nuchah n'chonah tachat kanfei ha-sh'chinah, b'ma-alot k'doshim u-t'horim k'zohar ha'rakiya maz-hirim et nish-mat ___ bat ___ she-halchah l'olamah, b'gan eiden t'hei menuchatah. Ana, ba-al ha-rachamim, hastireha b'seiter k'nafecha l'olamim, u-tzror bi-tzror hachayim et nishmatah, Adonai hu nachalatah, v'tanu-ach b'shalom al mishkavah, v'nomar amen.

God of compassion, grant perfect peace in Your sheltering Presence, among the holy and the pure who shine in the brightness of the firmament, to the soul of our dear ___ who has gone to her eternal rest. God of compassion, remember all her worthy deeds in the land of the living. May her soul be bound up in the bond of everlasting life. May God be her inheritance. May she rest in peace. And let us answer: Amen.

Things to remember:

1. Light the candle in the evening at sunset at the *Yahrtzeit* and on *Yizkor* days of holidays. Make sure it is a twenty-four-hour candle.

2. Even if the candle burns longer than twenty-four, let it burn. Do not extinguish it.

3. If you forget to light it in the evening, do so in the morning.

4. If you forgot to light the candle entirely, make a contribution to *tzedakah*.

Key words and phrases:

Yahrtzeit יָארְצַיט. Yiddish name for anniversary of one's death, known as *anos* among Sephardic Jews.

Yizkor יִזְכֹּר. Literally "May God remember," refers to service of memorial.

If you want to know more:

Ron Isaacs and Kerry Olitzky, *The Jewish Mourner's Handbook* (Hoboken, N.J., 1991).

How to Read a Tombstone
מַצֵּבָה

The source:

וַיַּצֵּב יַעֲקֹב מַצֵּבָה עַל־קְבֻרָתָהּ הִוא מַצֶּבֶת קְבֻרַת־רָחֵל עַד־הַיּוֹם:

"Over her grave Jacob set up a pillar. It is the pillar at Rachel's grave to this day" (Gen. 35:20).

What you need to know:

1. It is customary to erect a tombstone on the grave of the deceased.

2. There is no uniform practice with regard to the inscription on a stone. The stone today will often include the deceased's name in both Hebrew and English. In addition, it might also include dates of birth and death, sometimes in English and Hebrew as well.

3. The Ashkenazic practice is to place the Hebrew letters
    פ״נ, which stands for *po nitman,* meaning "here lies,"
    in front of the Hebrew name of a deceased individual.
    The Sephardic custom is to place the Hebrew letters
    מ״ק, which stands for *matzevet kevurat,* meaning "the
    tombstone of the grave."

    פֹּה נִטְמַן
    מַצֶּבֶת
    קְבוּרַת

4. Many tombstones have the Hebrew letters ת״נ״צ״ב״ה. This stands for *tehe nishmato tzerurah bitzror hachayim*, which means, "may his soul be bound in the bond of eternal life."

5. Some tombstones have pictorial Jewish symbols on them. Here are eight of the more common ones:

Star of David

The Menorah

The ewer or Levi Pitcher

The Yahrzeit

The Mosaic Decalogue

Kohanim Hands

The Scroll of the Pentateuch

The Lion

Things to remember:

1. A cemetery is a sacred environment. Respect it . . . and the memory of those who are buried there.

2. While a cemetery is like a park, it is no playground.

Key words and phrases:

Bet chaim בֵּית חַיִּים. Euphemism for "cemetery," literally "house of life."

Bet kevarot בֵּית קְבָרוֹת. Hebrew word for "cemetery"; alternatively, *bet chaim*, "house of life."

Matzevah מַצֵּיבָה. Hebrew word for "gravestone."

Unveiling. Consecration of a tombstone, usually occurring within a calendar year of a person's death.

If you want to know more:

Ron H. Isaacs and Kerry Olitzky, *The Jewish Mourner's Handbook* (Hoboken, N.J., 1991).

Isaac Klein, *A Guide to Jewish Religious Practice* (New York, 1979).

Isaac Klein, *A Time to be Born, a Time to Die* (New York, 1977).

Putting up a Mezuzah
מְזוּזָה

The source:

וּכְתַבְתָּם עַל־מְזֻזוֹת בֵּיתֶךָ וּבִשְׁעָרֶיךָ:

"Inscribe them on the doorposts of your house and on your gates" (Deut. 6:9, 11:20).

What you need to know:

1. Roll the parchment from the end to the beginning so that the word *Shema* is on top.

2. Place it in the *mezuzah* case.

3. Say the following blessings:

בָּרוּךְ אַתָּה יְיָ אֱלֹהֵינוּ מֶלֶךְ הָעוֹלָם אֲשֶׁר קִדְּשָׁנוּ בְּמִצְוֹתָיו וְצִוָּנוּ לִקְבּוֹעַ מְזוּזָה:

Baruch atah Adonai elohaynu melech ha'olam asher kidshanu bemitzvotav vetzivanu likboah mezuzah.

Praised are You, Adonai our God, Sovereign of the Universe, who has made us holy with mitzvot and instructed us to affix the *mezuzah*.

בָּרוּךְ אַתָּה יְיָ אֱלֹהֵינוּ מֶלֶךְ הָעוֹלָם שֶׁהֶחֱיָנוּ וְקִיְּמָנוּ וְהִגִּיעָנוּ לַזְּמַן הַזֶּה:

Baruch atah Adonai elohaynu melech ha'olam she-hecheyanu vekimanu vehigiyanu lazman hazeh.

Praised are You, Adonai our God, Sovereign of the Universe, who has kept us alive, sustained us, and helped us to reach this moment.

Things to remember:

1. The *mezuzah* literally means "doorpost" but is normally taken to refer to the case which holds the parchment and then is affixed to the doorpost.

2. A *mezuzah* should be placed on every doorpost in the house except for the bathrooms.

3. The *mezuzah* should be affixed to the upper third of the right-hand doorpost (as you enter) but no less than one handbreadth (the width of your hand) from the top.

4. On the parchment is written the *Shema Yisrael* and Deut 6:4-9, 11:13-31.

5. *Mezuzah* parchments should be checked twice every seven years.

6. When moving to a new home, leave your *mezuzot* for the new family—if it is Jewish. If not, take the *mezuzot* with you.

Key words and phrases:

Klaf קְלָף. The parchment inside the *mezuzah*.

If you want to know more:

Alfred Kolatch, *The Jewish Home Advisor* (Middle Village, N.Y., 1990).

More particulars:

Secret code on back of *mezuzah* parchment: *kuzo bemuchsaz kuzo*, which stands for *Adonai Elohenu Adonai*. כּוּזוּ בָּמוּכְסָז כּוּזוּ יְהֹוָה אֱלֹהֵנוּ יְהֹוָה

Shaddai: "Almighty God" and an acronym for *Shomer Daltot Yisrael*, meaning "protector of Israelite doors." שַׁדַּי שׁוֹמֵר דַּלְתוֹת יִשְׂרָאֵל

How to Dance the Hora
הוֹרָה

The source:

חֲלוּצִים

The early Jewish settlers in Israel, known as the *Chalutzim* (pioneers), brought the dance known as the hora from Eastern Europe.

What you need to know:

During the dance the participants form a circle and put their hands on each other's shoulders or hold each other's hands.

1 — Step right with right foot

2 — Place left foot behind right foot

3 — Step right with right foot

4 — Hop on right foot

5 — Step left with left foot

6 — Hop on left foot

Things to remember:

1. The hora is probably Judaism's most well-known circle dance.

Key words and phrases:

Rikud רִקּוּד. Dance.

If you want to know more:

Fred Berk, *Ha-Rikud: The Jewish Dance* (New York, 1972).

Making a Jewish Family Tree
מִשְׁפָּחָה

The source:

זֶה סֵפֶר תּוֹלְדֹת אָדָם:

"This is the book of the family record of humankind"
(Gen. 5:1).

What you need to know:

1. Look at family photograph albums with your parents
   and ask them to identify pictures of your relatives.
   Find out where and when they lived and how you are
   related to them.

2. Ask your grandparents, aunts, uncles, and cousins to
   tell you about your close relatives. Then ask them for
   this information about each person:
   a. Name
   b. Date of birth
   c. Place of birth
   d. Date of marriage
   e. Place of marriage
   f. Date of death
   g. Place of death

3. Once you have all of this information you can proceed
   to draw your family tree. Here is a sample chart that
   starts with you and traces your line back through
   your parents, grandparents, great-grandparents, and
   so on.

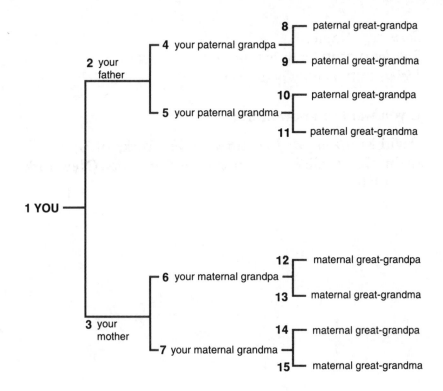

Who's who:

1. You
2. Father
3. Mother
4. Paternal grandfather
5. Paternal grandmother (family name)
6. Maternal grandfather
7. Maternal grandmother (family name)
8–11. Paternal great-grandparents
12–15. Maternal great-grandparents

Things to remember:

If you don't record your family history now, those who hold the key to family memory may be gone later on, when you want to know about your ancestors.

Key words and phrases:

L'dor vador לְדוֹר וָדוֹר. "From generation to generation."
Mishpacha מִשְׁפָּחָה. (Yiddish, *mishpacha*). Family.

Shem שֵׁם. Name.
Toledot תּוֹלְדוֹת. Family line.
Yichus יִחוּס. Family pedigree.

If you want to know more:

David Kranzler, *My Jewish Roots* (New York, 1979).
Arthur Kurzweil, *From Generation to Generation* (New York, 1980).

How to Visit the Sick
בִּקּוּר חוֹלִים

The source:

"These are the deeds which yield immediate fruit and continue to yield fruit in time to come: honoring parents, doing deeds of kindness, attending the house of study, visiting the sick . . . " (Babylonian Talmud Shabbat 127a).

What you need to know:

(based on *Shulchan Aruch, Yoreh Deah* 335):

1. It is a mitzvah to visit the sick. Feel free to visit even those who are not your relatives or friends.

2. Do not overdo your stay; lengthy visits often tire the patient.

3. Relatives and friends should visit as soon as the person becomes ill. More distant acquaintances may want to wait several days.

4. When visiting, always try to enter cheerfully.

5. Try not to speak about sad things to persons that you visit.

Things to remember:

1. Psalms which can be recited for someone who is ill: Psalms 6, 9, 13, 16, 17, 22, 23, 25, 30, 31, 32, 33, 37, 49, 55, 86, 88, 90, 91, 102, 103, 104, 118, 119, 142, 143.

2. Many synagogues and Jewish communities have *bikkur cholim* societies (or caring committees), which visit hospitals and nursing homes on a regular basis. If you have one, become an active member!

Key words and phrases:

Bikkur cholim בִּקּוּר חוֹלִים. The mitzvah of visiting the sick.

Bet cholim בֵּית חוֹלִים. Hebrew word for "hospital."

Mi sheberach מִי שֶׁבֵּרָךְ. Prayer for the sick, often recited in synagogue on behalf of person who is ill.

Vidui וִדּוּי. Confessional prayer often said by traditional Jew suffering from life-threatening illness.

If you want to know more:

Sharon and Michael Strassfeld, *The Third Jewish Catalogue* (Philadelphia, 1980).

Barbara Fortgang Summers, *Community Responsibility in the Jewish Tradition* (New York, 1978).

Tzedakah and
Doing Deeds of Kindness
צְדָקָה וּמַעֲשִׂים טוֹבִים

The sources:

עַל שְׁלֹשָׁה דְבָרִים הָעוֹלָם עוֹמֵד—עַל הַתּוֹרָה, וְעַל הָעֲבוֹדָה,
וְעַל גְּמִילוּת חֲסָדִים:

"The world rests on three things: Torah, worship and
the performance of good deeds" (Pirke Avot 1:2).

צֶדֶק צֶדֶק תִּרְדֹּף:

"Charity, charity, shall you pursue" (Deut. 16:20).

"These are things for which no measure is prescribed:
gleanings of the field, first fruits, festival offerings,
loving deeds of kindness, and the study of Torah.
These are things whose fruit a person enjoys in this
world and whose reward is stirred up in the World-
to-Come: honoring parents, doing deeds of kindness,
making peace, but the study of Torah is equal to them
all [because it leads to them]" (Peah 1:1).

What you need to know:

1. *Tzedakah,* often translated "charity," is derived from
   the Hebrew root *tzedek,* meaning "righteous" and
   "just." Giving *tzedakah* is the just and right thing to
   do.

   צְדָקָה
   צֶדֶק

2. *Gemilut chasadim* is the Hebrew term for "loving acts
   of kindness." Included in these acts are giving clothing to the needy, visiting the sick, comforting the
   mourner, and burying the dead.

   גְמִילוּת חֲסָדִים

3. When you give to someone or help someone, you should do it cheerfully and graciously.

4. It is considered best to help someone without the recipient knowing from whom the help is coming.

5. The highest form of a deed of kindness is to help a person to be self-supporting.

Key words and phrases:

Hachnasat orchim הַכְנָסַת אוֹרְחִים. "hospitality to strangers," an important act of kindness.
Pushke. (Yiddish). A charity box.
Tithe מַעֲשֵׂר. The giving of one tenth of your earnings to *tzedakah.*

If you want to know more:

Joseph Feinstein, *I Am My Brother's Keeper* (New York, 1970).
Jacob Neusner, *Tzedakah* (New York, 1982).
Danny Siegel, *Gym Shoes and Irises (Personalized Tzedakah).* (New York, 1982).

Finding the Meaning of Your Hebrew Name
שֵׁם עִבְרִי

The source:

נִבְחָר שֵׁם מֵעֹשֶׁר רָב:

"A good name is rather to be chosen than great riches" (Prov. 22:1).

What you need to know:

1. There are 2,800 personal names in the Bible, some of which are used to name children today. All Hebrew names have meanings.

2. Hebrew names with the prefix or suffix *el, eli, ya,* and *yahu* all refer to God.

   אֵל, אֱלִי
   יָה, יָהוּ

3. Many Hebrew names are nature names, such as Deborah (bee) or Jonah (dove).

   דְּבוֹרָה
   יוֹנָה

4. The usual American custom is to give a child both a secular and a Hebrew name. Sometimes the name may be the same in both Hebrew and English (like David, Leora, Shirah).

   דָּוִד
   לִיאוֹרָה
   שִׁירָה

5. If you want some advice about your particular Hebrew name you can ask a rabbi or cantor, or review one of the Hebrew-Name dictionaries listed in the "If you want to know more" section.

Some Biblical Names Commonly Used in English

אַהֲרֹן	Aaron	"singing" or "teaching"
אַבְרָהָם	Abraham	"father of a mighty nation"

אָדָם	Adam	"red earth"
עָמוֹס	Amos	"burdened"
בִּנְיָמִין	Benjamin	"son of my right hand"
דָּנִיאֵל	Daniel	"God is my judge"
דְּבוֹרָה	Deborah	"bee"
דִּינָה	Dinah	"judgment"
עִמָּנוּאֵל	Emanuel	"God is with us"
אֶסְתֵּר	Esther	"a star"
חַנָּה	Hannah	"merciful"
יַעֲקֹב	Jacob	"held by the heel"
יוֹנָתָן	Jonathan	"gift of God"
יוֹאֵל	Joel	"God is willing"
יוֹסֵף	Joseph	"He will increase"
יְהוּדִית	Judith	"praise"
מִיכָאֵל	Michael	"who is like God?"
מִרְיָם	Miriam	"bitter waters"
רָחֵל	Rachel	"ewe"
רִבְקָה	Rebekkah	"to bind"
רוּת	Ruth	"friendship"
שְׁמוּאֵל	Samuel	"God has listened"
שָׂרָה	Sarah	"princess"

Things to remember:

1. Most naming customs are just customs without a great deal of logic to them. There are no rules.

2. Different communities have different naming customs. For example, Ashkenazic Jews generally do not name their children in honor of a living person (only in memory of someone who is dead) but Sephardic Jews have a system (beginning with the paternal grandfather) of honoring living people by naming babies in their honor.

Key words and phrases:
Shem שֵׁם (plural, *shemot* שְׁמוֹת). Name.

If you want to know more:

Anita Diamant, *The Jewish Baby Book* (New York, 1988).
Heinrich and Eva Guggenheimer, *Jewish Family Names and Their Origins: An Etymological Dictionary* (Hoboken, N.J., 1992).
Benzion C. Kaganoff, *A Dictionary of Jewish Names and Their History* (New York, 1977).
Alfred J. Kolatch, *The Name Dictionary* (New York, 1967).

Sample entry from
*Jewish Family Names and Their Origins:
An Etymological Dictionary*

Schif, Schiff, Shief, Shieff, Shif, Shiff, שיף, "ship" (M.H.G., G.), transl. Hung. *hajó* (Hajos), Pol. *okręt* (Okrent), Russ. судно *sudno* (Sudnovsky); G. synonym Nauen. In Frankfurt/Main priestly family, descendants of Aberle Schiff ("ship", G.), son of Benedict Kahn ("boat", G.). Otherwise matr. from Shifke, Ashk. כ for Bibl. n. Shifra ("the beautiful", *Ex.* 1:15). Comp. Schiffeldrim, Shiffeldrim;bl (cf. M.H.G. *schipfe* "shovel, digging stick", *drum* "splinter, end piece"), Schiffenbauer (G. *Schiffbauer* "shipbuilder"), Schifer, Schiffer ("skipper" G.), Shifer, Shiffer, Schiffman, Schiffmann, Schifman ["skipper" M.H.G., cf. Sternik (Pol.), Steuerman (G.), Sturman (Russ.)], Shiffman, Shifman, Schifter, Shifter. Matr. of Shifra: Schifrin, Shifrin, Shifrine, Schifris, Shifris, Shifriss.

Synagogue Geography
בֵּית כְּנֶסֶת

The source:

There is no exact source regarding the synagogue as a
building for Jewish public prayer. It is widely believed
to have originated among the Babylonian exiles as
a substitute for the Temple, but probably coexisted
with the ancient Temple in an early form.

What you need to know:

1. There should be an ark in the east wall of the synagogue to contain the Torah scrolls.

2. There should be a *bimah* (platform) in the center from
which the Torah is read.

3. The synagogue should have windows. (This require-
ment comes from Daniel 6:11, which describes how
Daniel prayed by windows facing toward Jerusalem.)

Key words and phrases:

Aron hakodesh אֲרוֹן הַקֹּדֶשׁ. Holy ark, the receptacle on the
eastern wall that holds the Torah scrolls. It is located
there so that worshippers face Jerusalem when they
pray.

Bimah בִּימָה. Elevated platform from which the Torah is
read. In some synagogues it is placed in the center of
the sanctuary.

Ner tamid נֵר תָּמִיד. Eternal light, the light above the *aron
hakodesh* that is kept on daily throughout the year.
Its source is the *menorah* מְנוֹרָה (candelabrum) in the

118

ancient Tabernacle whose light burned continuously (Exod. 27:20–21).

Parochet פָּרוֹכֶת. Curtain that covers the *aron hakodesh.*

Torah תּוֹרָה. The scroll of the Five Books of Moses, written on parchment in Hebrew by a scribe. The parchment is placed on wooden handles known as *atzay chaim* (trees of life).

Who's who in the synagogue:

Rabbi רַב. Literally "teacher"; the rabbi gives the sermons, announces pages, gives the benediction, and many other things.

Chazzan חַזָן. The cantor; chants and sings the prayers, acting as *shaliach tzibbur,* or messenger/spokesperson of the congregation.

Gabbai גַבַּאי and *shamash.* Coordinates activities during the service, gives out the honors, assists the Torah reader, among other things.

Baal Koreh בַּעַל קוֹרֵא. Torah reader; reads from the Torah on the Sabbath, holidays, and Monday and Thursday mornings. This person is often the same as the *gabbai* or *shamash.*

Ushers. Persons who assist in keeping the decorum during a service. They will often give out prayer books and Bibles to the guests.

If you want to know more:

Encyclopaedia Judaica (Jerusalem, 1973) 15:579–627.

Richard Siegel, Michael Strassfeld, and Sharon Strassfeld, *The First Jewish Catalogue* (Philadelphia, 1973).

Thirty-Nine Labors Traditionally Prohibited on Shabbat
ל״ט מְלָאכוֹת

The source:

Babylonian Talmud, Shabbat 106a.

baking
bleaching
building
carrying in a public place
combing raw material
cutting to shape
demolishing
dyeing
erasing
extinguishing a fire
grinding
inserting thread in a loom
kindling a fire
kneading
marking out
plowing
reaping
removing the finished article
scraping
selecting
separating into threads
sewing
sheaf-making
sheep-shearing
sifting
skinning or flaying
slaughtering

sowing
spinning
tanning
tearing
the final hammer blow
threshing
trapping
tying a knot
untying a knot
weaving
winnowing
writing

Things to remember:

1. The Conservative, Reconstructionist, and Reform movements have different perspectives on these labors and their individual understanding of what is prohibited on Shabbat.

Key words and phrases:

Melacha מְלָאכָה. Form of work prohibited on the Sabbath.
Muktzeh מוּקְצָה. Precautionary measure by traditional Jews to not handle anything on the Sabbath pertaining to work, like tools or money.

If you want to know more:

I. Grunfeld. *The Sabbath* (New York, 1959).

The sources:

שִׁבְעַת יָמִים מַצּוֹת תֹּאכֵלוּ אַךְ בַּיּוֹם הָרִאשׁוֹן תַּשְׁבִּיתוּ שְּׂאֹר מִבָּתֵּיכֶם כִּי כָּל־אֹכֵל חָמֵץ וְנִכְרְתָה הַנֶּפֶשׁ הַהִוא מִיִּשְׂרָאֵל:

"For seven days, you shall eat unleavened bread . . . for seven days, there shall be no leavened products in your home for whoever eats *chametz* shall be cut off from the congregation" (Exod. 12:15, 19).

What you need to know:

חָמֵץ 1. *Chametz* is the leavened product that results when wheat, rye, barley, oats, or spelt (the "five grains") comes into contact with water for more than eighteen minutes. Therefore, all breads, pastries, cakes, cookies, and dry cereal are considered pure *chametz*.

2. In addition to these five grains, Askenazic Jews do not eat rice, corn, beans, peas, and peanuts on Pesach. Since flour can be made of these grains and baked into bread, it may lead to confusion, say the rabbis.

Things to remember:

1. When matzah is made from flour and water, it is carefully watched so that no water touches the flour prior to mixing for dough. Then it is mixed and baked in less than eighteen minutes.

Key words and phrases:

Chametz חָמֵץ. Unleavened products.
Matzah מַצָּה. Unleavened bread.

If you want to know more:

Isaac Klein, *A Guide to Jewish Religious Practice* (New York, 1979).

Morris Golumb, *Know Your Festivals and Enjoy Them* (New York, 1976).

Philip Goodman, *The Passover Anthology* (Philadelphia, 1961).

Prohibited/Permitted Foods
כָּשֵׁר—טְרֵפָה

The sources:

Leviticus 11:1–43; Exodus 23:19, 34:26; Deuteronomy 14:21.

Fowl

Prohibited	*Permitted*
bat	capon
cuckoo	chicken
eagle	dove
hawk	duck
heron	geese
kite	pigeon
lapwing	turkey
ostrich	
owl	
pelican	
stork	
swan	
vulture	

Fish and Seafood

Prohibited	*Permitted*
catfish	anchovy
eel	bluefish
porpoise	butterfish
shark	carp
whale	cod
clam	flounder

crab	fluke
frog	haddock
lobster	halibut
octopus	herring
oyster	mackerel
scallop	pike
shrimp	porgy
snail	red snapper
	salmon
	sardine
	seabass
	shad
	smelt
	sole
	trout
	tuna
	weakfish
	whitefish

Meat

1. All animals which chew their cud and have a split hoof are kosher. This includes cattle, sheep, goats, and deer. It excludes horses, donkeys, camels, and pigs.

2. Meat must be killed according to the laws of *shechitah*.

3. Once the beast has been slaughtered, it must be properly salted (to remove excess blood).

Eggs

1. Eggs from non-kosher birds are not kosher.

2. Eggs with bloodspots are not kosher.

Things to remember:

1. Kashrut refers to
   a. proper
   b. foods that can be eaten
   c. separation of milk and meat

2. Because of the nature of liver, its kashrut is extra difficult to determine. See your rabbi.

3. There are lots of new fish being sold in the market today. If you are unsure whether something is kosher, consult your rabbi.

Key words and phrases:

Asur אָסוּר. Prohibited.
Mutar מוּתָּר. Permitted.
Shehitah שְׁחִיטָה. Process of ritual slaughter.
Shochet שׁוֹחֵט. The one who does the ritual slaughter.
Treif טְרֵפָה. Unfit.

If you want to know more:

Seymour Freedman, *The Book of Kashruth* (New York, 1970).

Isaac Klein, *A Guide to Jewish Religious Practice* (New York, 1979).

Instant Information
Rules for Kashrut
חֻקֵּי כַּשְׁרוּת

The sources:

לֹא־תְבַשֵּׁל גְּדִי בַּחֲלֵב עִמּוֹ:

a. "You shall not cook a kid in its mother's milk" (Exod. 23:19).

וְהִבְדַּלְתֶּם בֵּין־הַבְּהֵמָה הַטְּהֹרָה לַטְּמֵאָה:

b. "You shall set apart the (ritually) clean beast from the unclean" (Lev. 20:25).

וּבָשָׂר בַּשָּׂדֶה טְרֵפָה לֹא תֹאכֵלוּ לַכֶּלֶב תַּשְׁלִכוּן אֹתוֹ:

c. "You must not eat flesh torn by beasts" (Exod. 22:30).

לֹא תֹאכְלוּ כָל־נְבֵלָה:

d. "You shall not eat anything that died a natural death" (Deut. 14:21).

What you need to know:

1. The basic requirements for a kosher kitchen are:
   a. There should be nothing non-kosher in it.
   b. Meat and dairy products and utensils need to be separated.

2. Permitted foods include the following:
   a. All fresh fruits and vegetables are kosher.
   b. All unprocessed grains and cereals are kosher.
   c. All milk and most dairy products, including hard cheese, are kosher according to the Rabbinical Assembly of America, an organization of Conservative rabbis.

d. Eggs from kosher fowl are kosher.

e. Fish that have fins and scales are kosher.

f. For an animal to be kosher, it must have split hooves, chew its cud, and be slaughtered in a kosher slaughtering house.

g. Most domestic fowl are kosher.

h. According to the Rabbinical Assembly of America, all machine-made wines are kosher.

3. Conservative Jews and some Reform Jews wait three or six hours after eating meat before eating dairy things.

Things to remember:

1. Kosher symbols: identifying symbols placed on various food products by the manufacturer identifying the product as certified kosher.

    Sample symbols include the following:

    Union of Orthodox Jewish Congregations

    Kosher Supervision Service

    Organized Kashrus Laboratories

Key words and phrases:

Chalaf חַלָף. Razor-sharp knife used by *shochet* שׁוֹחֵט in slaughtering animals.

Chalav Yisrael חָלָב יִשְׂרָאֵל. Literally "Israelite milk," refers to milk that has been under careful supervision by a Jew from the moment of milking to the time of bottling.

Fleishig (Yiddish). A product deriving from meat (*besari* in Hebrew).

Glatt kosher גְלָאט כָּשֵׁר. Literally "smooth," refers to animals whose lungs are smooth with no punctures. Generally, this refers to meat that was inspected to be kosher on slaughtering and does not require further inspection.

Kasher כָּשֵׁר. Fit and proper to eat.

Kashering. The process of making utensils kosher for use.

Kashrut כַּשְׁרוּת. The system of the Jewish dietary laws.

Milchig (Yiddish). A dairy-based food (*chalavi* חַלָבִי in Hebrew).

Nevelah נְבֵלָה. Refers to an animal that dies by itself. Such an animal is non-kosher.

Pareve פַּרְוֶע. Something neutral, neither meat nor dairy. (All fish, eggs, fruits, vegetables, and grains are pareve.)

Tref טְרֵפָה. The opposite of kosher. Non-kosher food that is forbidden to be eaten by those who observe the laws of kashrut.

If you want to know more:

Samuel H. Dresner and Seymour Siegel, *The Jewish Dietary Laws* (New York, 1982).

James M. Lebeau, *The Jewish Dietary Laws: Sanctify Life* (New York, 1983).

What you need to know:

Hebrew Name		English Name
	TORAH	TORAH
בְּרֵאשִׁית	Bereishit	Genesis
שְׁמוֹת	Shemot	Exodus
וַיִּקְרָא	Vayikra	Leviticus
בַּמִדְבָּר	Bamidbar	Numbers
דְּבָרִים	Devarim	Deuteronomy
	NEVI'IM	PROPHETS
יְהוֹשֻׁעַ	Yehoshua	Joshua
שׁוֹפְטִים	Shofetim	Judges
שְׁמוּאֵל א׳	Shmuel Aleph	I Samuel
שְׁמוּאֵל ב׳	Shmuel Bet	II Samuel
מְלָכִים א׳	Melachim Aleph	I Kings
מְלָכִים ב׳	Melachim Bet	II Kings
יְשַׁעְיָה	Yeshayah	Isaiah
יִרְמְיָה	Yermiyah	Jeremiah
יְחֶזְקֵאל	Yechezkel	Ezekiel
הוֹשֵׁעַ	Hoshaya	Hosea
יוֹאֵל	Yoel	Joel
עָמוֹס	Amos	Amos
עוֹבַדְיָה	Ovadyah	Obadiah
יוֹנָה	Yonah	Jonah
מִיכָה	Michah	Micah
נַחוּם	Nachum	Nahum
חֲבַקּוּק	Chabakkuk	Habakkuk
צְפַנְיָה	Tzephanyah	Zephaniah

חַגַּי	Chaggai	Haggai
זְכַרְיָה	Zecharyah	Zecharyah
מַלְאָכִי	Malachi	Malachi
	KETUVIM	WRITINGS
תְּהִלִּים	Tehillim	Psalms
מִשְׁלֵי	Mishlei	Proverbs
אִיוֹב	Eeyov	Job
שִׁיר הַשִּׁירִים	Shir Ha-shirim	Song of Songs
רוּת	Root	Ruth
אֵיכָה	Eicha	Lamentations
קֹהֶלֶת	Kohelet	Ecclesiastes
אֶסְתֵּר	Ester	Esther
דָּנִיאֵל	Daniel	Daniel
עֶזְרָה	Ezra	Ezra
נְחֶמְיָה	Nechemyah	Nehemiah
דִּבְרֵי הַיָּמִים א׳	Divrey Hayamim Aleph	I Chronicles
דִּבְרֵי הַיָּמִים ב׳	Divrey Hayamim Bet	II Chronicles

Things to remember:

1. English names usually communicate themes. Hebrew names usually refer to the first large words in the opening section of the particular book.

Key words and phrases:

Chumash חוּמָשׁ. From the word for "five," *chamesh* חָמֵשׁ; the first five books of the Bible.

Tanach תַּנַ״ךְ. Hebrew name for entire Bible, acronym derived from the names of the Bible's three divisions: Torah תּוֹרָה, Nevi'im נְבִיאִים (Prophets), and Ketuvim כְּתוּבִים (Writings).

If you want to know more:

Azriel Eisenberg, *The Book of Books* (New York, 1976).
Sylvan Schwartzman and Jack Spiro, *The Living Bible* (New York, 1966).

More particulars:

Masoretic text. Authoritative Hebrew text of the Bible produced by the scribes called the Masoretes.

Instant Information
Parashat Hashavuah: Weekly Torah/Haftarah Readings
פָּרָשַׁת הַשָּׁבוּעַ

The source:

Babylonian Talmud, Megilla 29b.

What you need to know:

Name		Torah Text	Prophetic Reading
Bereishit	Genesis	1:1-6:8	Isaiah 42:5-43:11 (42:5-21)
Noach		6:9-11:32	Isaiah 54:1-55:5 (54:1-10)
Lech Lecha		12:1-17:27	Isaiah 40:27-41:16
Vayera		18:1-22:24	II Kings 4:1-37 (4:1-23)
Chayei Sarah		23:1-25:18	I Kings 1:1-31
Toledot		25:19-28:9	Malachi 1:1-2:7
Vayetzei		28:10-32:3	Hosea 12:12-14:10 (11:7-12:12)
Vayishlach		32:4-36:43	Hosea 11:17-12:12 (Obadiah 1:1-21)
Vayeshev		37:1-40:23	Amos 2:6-3:8
Miketz		41:1-44:17	I Kings 3:15-4:1
Vayigash		44:18-47:27	Ezekiel 37:15-25
Vayechi		47:28-50:26	I Kings 2:1-12
Shemot	Exodus	1:1-6:1	Isaiah 27:6-28:13; 29:22-23 (Jeremiah 1:1-2:3)
Vaeyra		6:2-9:35	Ezekiel 28:25-29:21
Bo		10:1-13:16	Jeremiah 46:13-28

Beshallach		13:17-17:16	Judges 4:4-5:31 (5:1-31)
Yitro		18:1-20:23	Isaiah 6:1-7:6; 9:5-6
			(6:1-13)
Mishpatim		21:1-24:18	Jeremiah 34:8-22; 33:25-26
Terumah		25:1-27:19	I Kings 5:26-6:13
Tetzaveh		27:20-30:10	Ezekiel 43:10-27
Ki Tisa		30:11-34:35	I Kings 18:1-39
			(18:20-39)
Vayakhel		35:1-38:20	I Kings 7:40-50 (7:13:26)
Pekudei		38:21-40:38	I Kings 7:51-8:21
			(7:40-50)
Vayikra	Leviticus	1:1-5:26	Isaiah 43:21-44:23
Tzav		6:1-8:36	Jeremiah 7:21-8:3; 9:22-23
Shemini		9:1-11:47	II Samuel 6:1-7:17
			(6:1-19)
Tazria		12:1-13:59	II Kings 4:42-5:19
Metzora		14:1-15:33	II Kings 7:3-20
Acharei Mot		16:1-18:30	Ezekiel 22:1-19 (22:1-16)
Kedoshim		19:1-20:27	Amos 9:7-15
			(Ezekiel 20:2-20)
Emor		21:1-24:23	Ezekiel 44:15-31
Behar		25:1-26:2	Jeremiah 32:6-27
Bechukotai		26:3-27:34	Jeremiah 16:19-17:14
Bemidbar	Numbers	1:1-4:20	Hosea 2:1-22
Naso		4:21-7:89	Judges 13:2-25
Behaalotecha		8:1-12:16	Zechariah 2:14-4:7
Shelach		13:1-15:41	Joshua 2:1-24
Korach		16:1-18:32	I Samuel 11:14-12:22
Chukat		19:1-22:1	Judges 11:1-33
Balak		22:2-25:9	Micah 5:6-6:8
Pinchas		25:10-30:1	I Kings 18:46-19:21
Mattot		30:2-32:42	Jeremiah 1:1-2:3
Masey		33:1-36:13	Jeremiah 2:4-28; 3:4
			(2:4-28; 4:1-2)
Devarim	Deuteronomy	1:1-3:22	Isaiah 1:1-27
Va-etchanan		3:23-7:11	Isaiah 40:1-26

Ekev		7:12-11:25	Isaiah 49:14-51:3
Re'eh		11:26-16:17	Isaiah 54:11-55:5
Shofetim		16:18-21:9	Isaiah 51:12-52:12
Ki Tetze		21:10-25:19	Isaiah 54:1-10
Ki Tavo		26:1-29:8	Isaiah 60:1-22
Nitzavim		29:9-30:20	Isaiah 61:10-63:9
Vayelech		31:1-30	Isaiah 55:6-56:8
Haazinu		32:1-52	II Samuel 22:1-51
Vezot Ha-berachah		33:1-34:12	Joshua 1:1-18 (1:1-9)

Note: parentheses indicate Sephardic ritual

Special Readings

Rosh Hashanah	1st Day	Genesis 21:1-34; Numbers 29:1-6	I Samuel 1:1-2:10
	2nd Day	Genesis 22:1-24; Numbers 29:1-6	Jeremiah 31:2-20
Shabbat Shuvah		Weekly portion	Hosea 14:2-10; Micah 7:18-20 or Hosea 14:2-10; (Hosea 14:2-10; Micah 7:18-20)
Yom Kippur	Morning	Leviticus 16:1-34; Numbers 29:7-11	Isaiah 57:14-58:14
Sukkot	1st Day	Leviticus 22:26-23:44; Numbers 29:12-16	Zechariah 14:1-21
	2nd Day	Leviticus 22:26-23:44; Numbers 29:12-16	I Kings 8:2-21
Shabbat Chol Hamoed Sukkot		Exodus 33:12-34:26; Daily portion from Numbers 29	Ezekiel 38:18-39:16
	8th Day	Deuteronomy 14:22-16:17; Numbers 29:35-30:1	I Kings 8:56-66
Simchat Torah		Deuteronomy 33:1-34:12;	Joshua 1:1-18

		Genesis 1:1-2:3	(1:1-9)
		Numbers 29:35-30:1	
1st Shabbat Chanukah		Weekly and Chanukah portions	Zechariah 2:14-4:7
2nd Shabbat Chanukah		Weekly and Chanukah portions	I Kings 7:40-50
Shabbat Shekalim		Weekly portion; Exodus 30:11-16	II Kings 12:1-17 (11:17-12:17)
Shabbat Zachor		Weekly portion; Deuteronomy 25:17-19	I Samuel 15:2-34 (15:1-34)
Shabbat Parah		Weekly portion; Numbers 19:1-22	Ezekiel 36:16-38 (36:16-36)
Shabbat Hachodesh		Weekly portion; Exodus 12:1-20	Ezekiel 45:16-46:18 (45:18-46:15)
Shabbat Hagadol		Weekly portion	Malachi 3:4-24
Pesach	1st Day	Exodus 12:21-51; Numbers 28:16-25	Joshua 3:5-7; 5:2-6:1; 6:27 (5:2-6:1)
	2nd Day	Leviticus 22:26-23:44; Numbers 28:16-25	II Kings 23:1-9; 21-25
Shabbat Pesach		Exodus 33:12-34:26; Numbers 28:19-25	Ezekiel 36:37-37:14 (37:1-14)
	7th Day	Exodus 13:17-15:26; Numbers 28:19-25	II Samuel 22:1-51
	8th Day	Deut. 15:19-16:17; (on Shabbat 14:22-16:17) Numbers 28:19-25	Isaiah 10:32-12:6
Shavuot	1st Day	Exodus 19:11-:23 Numbers 28:26-31	Ezekiel 1:1-28; 3:12

	2nd Day	Deut. 15:19-16:17	Habakkuk 3:1-19
		(on Shabbat 14:22-6:17)	(2:20-3:19)
		Numbers 28:26-31	
Tisha B'av	Morning	Deut. 4:25-40	Jeremiah 8:13-9:23
	Afternoon	Exodus 32:11-14 34:1-10	Isaiah 55:6-56:8
Shabbat Rosh Chodesh		Weekly portion	Isaiah 66:1-24
Shabbat immediately preceding Rosh Chodesh		Weekly portion	I Samuel 20:18-42

Things to remember:

1. Number of *aliyot*
   Weekdays: three
   Rosh Chodesh/Chol Hamoed: four
   Holidays: five
   Yom Kippur: six
   Shabbat: seven

2. In some cases, the Reform movement has adjusted the cycle of Torah/Haftarah readings especially for the High Holidays.

Key words and phrases:

Derasha דְּרָשָׁה. Torah commentary or sermon.
Devar Torah דְּבַר תּוֹרָה. Torah lesson.
Parashat hashavuah פָּרָשַׁת הַשָּׁבוּעַ. Weekly Torah reading.
Sidrah סִדְרָה. Generally used today interchangeably with *parashat hashavuah,* the Torah portion read any particular week.

If you want to know more:

Azriel Eisenberg, *The Book of Books* (New York, 1976).
Sylvan Schwartzman and Jack Spiro, *The Living Bible* (New York, 1966).

The Hebrew (Luni-Solar) Calendar
לוּחַ עִבְרִי

The source:

הַחֹדֶשׁ הַזֶּה לָכֶם רֹאשׁ חֳדָשִׁים.

This month should be the first of months for you (Exodus 12:1).

What you need to know:

Months of the Year

נִיסָן	**Nisan**
אִיָּיר	**Iyar**
סִיוָן	**Sivan**
תַּמּוּז	**Tammuz**
אָב	**Av**
אֱלוּל	**Elul**
תִּשְׁרֵי	**Tishri**
(מַר) חֶשְׁוָן	**(Mar) Cheshvan**
כִּסְלֵו	**Kislev**
טֵבֵת	**Tevet**
שְׁבָט	**Shevat**
אַדָר	**Adar**

Holidays/Festivals

רֹאשׁ הַשָּׁנָה	**Rosh Hashanah**	**1 Tishri**
יוֹם כִּפּוּר	**Yom Kippur**	**10 Tishri**

138

סוכּוֹת	**Sukkot**	**15 Tishri**
שְׁמִינִי עֲצֶרֶת/	**Shemini Atzeret/**	**22/23 Tishri**
שִׂמְחַת תּוֹרָה	**Simchat Torah**	
חֲנוּכָּה	**Chanukah**	**25 Kislev-2/3 Tevet**
ט״וּ בִּשְׁבָט	**Tu Bishevat**	**15 Shevat**
פּוּרִים	**Purim**	**14 Adar**
פֶּסַח	**Pesach**	**15 Nisan-23 Nisan**
יוֹם הַשּׁוֹאָה	**Yom Hashoah**	**27 Nisan**
יוֹם הָעַצְמָאוּת	**Yom Ha-atzmaut**	**5 Iyar**
שָׁבוּעוֹת	**Shavuot**	**6 Sivan**
תִּשְׁעָה בְּאָב	**Tisha B'av**	**9 Av**

Things to remember:

1. Since the Reform movement accepts the precision of the mathematical formula used to anticipate holidays in advance, the three pilgrimage festivals are celebrated for one day less, as is Rosh Hashanah. Thus, Simchat Torah may be celebrated one day earlier in Reform congregations.

2. During leap year, a full month (Adar II) is added.   אֲדָר ב׳

3. Cheshvan is sometimes called Marcheshvan.

Key words and phrases:

Luach לוּחַ. Calendar.
Shana me-uberet שָׁנָה מְעוּבֶּרֶת. Hebrew leap year.

If you want to know more:

Raymond Zwerin, *The Jewish Calendar* (Denver, 1975).

More particulars:

Symbols of the Jewish zodiac.

Nisan—lamb; Iyar—ox; Sivan—twins; Tammuz—crab;
Av—lion; Elul—young maiden; Tishri—scale;
Cheshvan—scorpion; Kislev—rainbow; Tevet—goat;
Shevat—vessel filled with water; Adar—fish.

Phases of the Moon

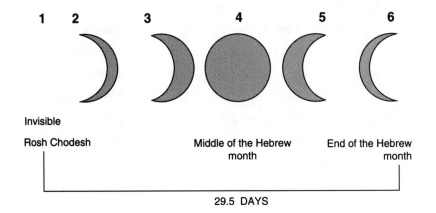

Instant Information
Alef-bet
א־ב

What you need to know:

Name	Print	Script	Sound	Numerical Value
Aleph	א	ⲓⲥ	silent	1
Bet	בּ	ⲁ	B	2
(Vet)	ב	ⲁ	(V)	(2)
Gimel	ג	ⲇ	G	3
Dalet	ד	ⲣ	D	4
Heh	ה	ⲏ	H	5
Vav	ו	/	V	6
Zayin	ז	ⲍ	Z	7
Chet	ח	ⲛ	CH	8
Tet	ט	ⲩ	T	9
Yod	י	'	Y	10
Kaf	כּ	ⲟ	K	20
(Chaf)	כ	ⲟ	(CH)	(20)
(Final Chaf)	ך	ⲣ	(CH)	(20)
Lamed	ל	ⲥ	L	30
Mem	מ	ⲛ	M	40
(Final Mem)	ם	ⲟ	(M)	(40)
Nun	נ	ⳑ	N	50
(Final Nun)	ן	|	(N)	(50)
Samech	ס	0	S	60
Ayin	ע	ⲭ	silent (guttural)	70
Peh	פּ	ⲟ	P	80
(Feh)	פ	ⲟ	(F)	(80)
(Final Feh)	ף	ⳑ	(F)	(80)
Tzadee	צ	3	TZ	90
(Final Tzadee)	ץ	ⳑ	(TZ)	(90)
Kuf	ק	ⲣ	K	100

Resh	ר	ﬧ	R	200
Shin	שׁ	℮	SH	300
(Sin)	שׂ	℮	S	(300)
Tav	ת	ﬨ	T	400

Vowels

Name	Block/Script	Sound
kametz	ָ	ah
patach	ַ	ah
tzere	ֵ	ay
segol	ֶ	eh
shooruk	וּ	oo
kubutz	ֻ	oo
cholem	וֹ	o
chiriq	ִ	ee
sheva	ְ	ih/silent

Things to remember:

1. When a *patach* is under a *chet* ח at the end of a word, the vowel is sounded before the letter.

2. When a *sheva* is added to a vowel, the word *chataf* is added to the vowel name.

Key words and phrases:

Sofer סוֹפֵר. Scribe.

Tagin תָּגִין. (singular, *tag*). Aramaic word for special designs resembling crowns used by scribes on selected letters (שעטנזגץ).

If you want to know more:

Lawrence Kushner, *The Book of Letters, the Mystical Alef Bet* (Woodstock, Vt. 1990).

David Diringer, *The Story of the Aleph Bet* (New York, 1960).

Instant Information

Basic Modern Hebrew Vocabulary

עִבְרִית מוֹדֶרְנִית

What you need to know:

father	אַבָּא	abba
mother	אִמָא	ima
grandfather	סַבָּא	saba
grandmother	סַבְתָּא	savta
uncle	דוֹד	dod
aunt	דוֹדָה	doda
brother	אָח	ach
sister	אָחוֹת	achot
boy	יֶלֶד	yeled
girl	יַלְדָה	yalda
family	מִשְׁפָּחָה	mishpacha
house	בַּיִת	bayit
synagogue	בֵּית כְּנֶסֶת	bet knesset
store	חֲנוּת	chanut
car	מְכוֹנִית	mechonit
school	בֵּית סֵפֶר	bet sefer
teacher	מוֹרָה(m) (f) מוֹרָה	moreh (m) morah (f)
restaurant	מִסְעָדָה	misada

Hebrew Phrases

hello, goodbye, peace unto you	שָׁלוֹם	shalom

how are you (m)	מַה שְׁלוֹמְךָ	*mah shlomcha*
how are you (f)	מַה שְׁלוֹמֵךְ	*mah shlomech*
what's your name (m)	מַה שִׁמְךָ	*ma shimcha*
what's your name (f)	מַה שְׁמֵךְ	*ma shmech*
all is okay	הַכֹּל בְּסֵדֶר	*hakol b'seder*
good morning	בֹּקֶר טוֹב	*boker tov*
good evening	עֶרֶב טוֹב	*erev tov*
good night	לַיְלָה טוֹב	*liala tov*
please	בְּבַקָשָׁה	*bevakasha*
thank you	תּוֹדָה	*todah*
really!	בֶּאֱמֶת	*be'emet*
what time is it	מַה הַשָׁעָה	*mah ha-shaah*
too bad	חֲבָל	*chaval*
so so	כָּכָה כָּכָה	*kacha kacha*
excuse me	סְלַח לִי	*slach lee*
right	יְמִינָה	*yemina*
left	שְׂמֹאלָה	*smolah*
up	לְמַעֲלָה	*lemalah*
down	לְמַטָּה	*lemata*
quiet	שֶׁקֶט	*sheket*
see you again	לְהִתְרָאוֹת	*l'hitraot*
yes	כֵּן	*ken*
no	לֹא	*lo*

If you want to know more:

Reuven Alcalay, *The Complete Hebrew-English English-Hebrew Dictionary,* 2 vol. (Jerusalem, 1981).

Instant Information
Greetings for Shabbat, Holiday and Everyday

Shabbat

Shabbat Shalom שַׁבָּת שָׁלוֹם. Sabbath greetings.
Gut Shabbos (Yiddish). Good Sabbath.

After Havdalah

Shavuah tov שָׁבוּעַ טוֹב. Good week.
A gut voch (Yiddish). A good week.

General Holiday

Gut yontif (from *yom tov*) (Yiddish). Happy holiday.
Chag sameach חַג שָׂמֵחַ. Happy holiday.

Rosh Hashanah

Shanah tovah שָׁנָה טוֹבָה. A good year.
Shanah tovah u'metukah שָׁנָה טוֹבָה וּמְתוּקָה. A good sweet year.
Le'shanah tovah tikatayvu לְשָׁנָה טוֹבָה תִּכָּתֵבוּ. May you be inscribed [in the book of life] for a good year.
Gut yohr (Yiddish). Good year.

Between Rosh Hashanah and Yom Kippur

G'mar chatimah tovah גְּמַר חֲתִימָה טוֹבָה. (shortened to *G'mar tov* גְּמַר טוֹב). May your inscription [in the book of life] be concluded.
Tzom kal צוֹם קַל. An easy fast (said prior to Yom Kippur after Rosh Hashanah).

Yom Kippur

Le'shanah tovah tikatayvu ve'techataymu לְשָׁנָה טוֹבָה תִּכָּתֵבוּ וְתֵחָתֵמוּ. May you be inscribed and sealed [in the book of life] for a good year.

Sukkot, Pesach, Shavuot

Moadim lesimcha מוֹעֲדִים לְשִׂמְחָה. Happy holiday. (Response: *Chagim uzmanim lesasson* חַגִּים וּזְמַנִּים לְשָׂשׂוֹן, may your holiday be a happy one.)

Daily Greetings

Boker tov בֹּקֶר טוֹב. Good morning (response: *boker or* בֹּקֶר אוֹר "the morning light").
Erev tov עֶרֶב טוֹב. Good evening.
Laila tov לַיְלָה טוֹב. Good night.
Lihitraot לְהִתְרָאוֹת. See you later.
Shalom שָׁלוֹם. Hello, goodbye, may you be at peace.

Things to remember:

1. Don't tell people *shanah tovah tikatayvu* after Rosh Hashanah. It's sort of an insult which implies that they were not inscribed in the book of life during Rosh Hashanah.

2. On somber fast days like Yom Kippur, greetings are generally not exchanged.

3. After you have had an *aliyah* or addressed the congregation, people may say *yasher koach*, "May your strength increase."
   (response *Baruch tiheyeh*: May it blessedly come to be.)

4. Upon leaving the cemetery, friends form two parallel columns to say the following to the mourner: *Hamakom yinachem etchem betoch shear avelai tziyon Verushalayim:* May God comfort you among the other mourners for Zion and Jerusalem.

146

Instant Information
The Ten Commandments
עֲשֶׂרֶת הַדִּבְּרוֹת

The sources:

Exodus 20:1–17; Deuteronomy 5:1–18.

What you need to know:

1. I am Adonai your God, who brought you out of the land of Egypt, out of the house of bondage.

2. You shall have no other gods in place of Me, nor make for yourself any idols.

3. You shall not speak God's name for no purpose.

4. Remember the Sabbath Day and keep it holy.

5. Honor your father and mother.

6. Do not murder.

7. Do not commit adultery.

8. Do not steal.

9. Do not bear false witness against your neighbor.

10. Do not covet anything that your neighbor owns.

Things to remember:

1. The Ten Commandments are repeated in a slightly different way in Exodus and Deuteronomy.

2. When the Ten Commandments are read in the synagogue, the entire congregation stands.

Key words and phrases:

Aseret hadibrot עֲשֶׂרֶת הַדִּבְּרוֹת. Literally, ten spoken words.
Luchot habrit לוּחוֹת הַבְּרִית. Literally, tablets of the covenant.

If you want to know more:

Abraham Chaim Feuer, *Aseres Hadibros* (New York, 1981).
Isaac Klein, *The Ten Commandments in a Changing World* (Jerusalem, 1965).

Instant Information
Thirteen Principles of Faith
שְׁלשׁ עֶשְׂרֵה עִקֲרֵי אֱמוּנָה

The source:

Maimonides' Commentary on the Mishnah.

What you need to know:

1. I believe with perfect faith that the Creator, blessed be Your name, is the Author and Guide of everything that has been created, and that God alone has made, does make, and will make all things.

2. I believe with perfect faith that the Creator, blessed be Your name, is a Unity, and that there is no unity in any manner like unto You, and that You alone are our God, who was, is, and will be.

3. I believe with perfect faith that the Creator, blessed be Your name, is not a body, and that You are free from all the accidents of matter, and that You have not any form whatsoever.

4. I believe with perfect faith that the Creator, blessed be Your name, is the first and the last.

5. I believe with perfect faith that to the Creator, blessed be Your name, and to You alone, it is right to pray, and that it is not right to pray to any being besides You.

6. I believe with perfect faith that all the words of the prophets are true.

7. I believe with perfect faith that the prophecy of Moses

our teacher, peace be unto him, was true, and that he was the chief of the prophets, both of those that preceded and of those that followed him.

8. I believe with perfect faith that the whole Torah, now in our possession, is the same that was given to Moses our teacher, peace be unto him.

9. I believe with perfect faith that this Torah will not be changed, and that there will never be any other law from the Creator, blessed be Your name.

10. I believe with perfect faith that the Creator, blessed be Your name, knows every deed of the human race and all of their thoughts, as it is said, "It is You who fashions the hearts of them all, that give heed to all their deeds."

11. I believe with perfect faith that the Creator, blessed be Your name, rewards those that keep Your *mitzvot,* and punishes those who transgress them.

12. I believe with perfect faith in the coming of the Messiah, and, though Messiah tarry, I will wait daily for the coming of the Messiah.

13. I believe with perfect faith that there will be a resurrection of the dead at the time when it shall please the Creator blessed be Your name, and exalted be the remembrance of You forever and ever.

Things to remember:

1. This is one man's attempt at getting to the essential system of Judaism, but there is no basic creed or dogma in Judaism.

יִגְדַּל 2. The *Yigdal* hymn is based on these thirteen principles. It was written as a mnemonic (memory) device to help people remember them by singing them.

3. Moses Maimondes (or Moses ben Maimon, also known by the acronym RaMBaM) was among the greatest Jewish philosophers. He lived 1135–1204 in Spain and later Egypt. His major works include the *Guide for the Perplexed* (*Moreh Nevuchim*) and *Mishneh Torah*.

Key words and phrases:

Ani maamin אֲנִי מַאֲמִין. I believe.
Emunah אֱמוּנָה. Faith.

If you want to know more:

Aryeh Kaplan, *Maimonides' Principles* (New York, 1975).

Maimonides'
Eight Degrees of Tzedakah
צְדָקָה

The source:

Mishneh Torah of Moses Maimonides.

What you need to know:

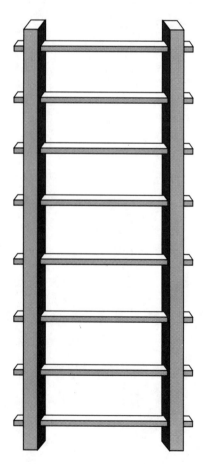

1. The person who gives reluctantly and with regret.

2. The person who gives graciously, but less than one should.

3. The person who gives what one should, but only after being asked.

4. The person who gives before being asked.

5. The person who gives without knowing to whom one gives, although the recipient knows the identity of the donor.

6. The person who gives without making one's identity known.

7. The person who gives without knowing to whom one gives. The recipient does not know from whom he receives.

8. The person who helps another to support oneself by a gift or a loan or by finding employment for that person, thus helping that person to become self-supporting.

Things to remember:

1. The dignity of the poor must always be respected.

2. Helping people to help themselves is the greatest form of *tzedakah*.

Key words and phrases:

Tzedakah צְדָקָה. Righteous giving, charity.

If you want to know more:

Joseph Feinstein, *I Am My Brother's Keeper* (New York, 1970).

Joel Grishaver and Beth Huppin, *Tzedakah, Gemilut Chasadim and Ahavah* (Denver, 1983).

Jacob Neusner, *Tzedakah* (Chappaqua, N.Y., 1982).

Instant Information
Singing Hatikvah
הַתִּקְוָה

The source:

The text was written by poet Naphtali Herz Imber, probably in Jassy, Romania, in 1878, and was inspired by the founder of Petach Tikvah (near Tel Aviv). The music, prepared by Samuel Cohen, is based on a Romanian folk song.

What you need to know:

כָּל־עוֹד בַּלֵּבָב פְּנִימָה
נֶפֶשׁ יְהוּדִי הוֹמִיָּה
וּלְפַאֲתֵי מִזְרָח קָדִימָה
עַיִן לְצִיּוֹן צוֹפִיָּה.
עוֹד לֹא אָבְדָה תִּקְוָתֵנוּ
הַתִּקְוָה בַּת שְׁנוֹת אַלְפַּיִם
לִהְיוֹת עַם חָפְשִׁי בְּאַרְצֵנוּ
אֶרֶץ צִיּוֹן וִירוּשָׁלָיִם.

Kol od ba-levav pnimah
Nefesh Yehudi homiyyah
U-lefa'atei mizrach kadimah
Ayin le-Tziyyon tzofiyah

Od lo avdah tikvatenu
Ha-tikvah bat shenot alpayim
Lihyot am chofshi be-artzenu
Eretz Tziyyon viY-rushalayim

As long as deep in the heart
The soul of a Jew yearns
And towards the East
An eye looks to Zion

154

Our hope is not yet lost
The hope of two thousand years
To be a free people in our land
The land of Zion and Jerusalem

Things to remember:

1. Always stand when Hatikvah is played or sung.

2. In religious Zionist families, there is a tradition of singing Psalm 126 during *zemirot* (Sabbath table songs) to the melody of Hatikvah.

Key words and phrases:

Hatikvah הַתִּקְוָה. The hope.

If you want to know more:

Encyclopaedia Judaica (Jerusalem, 1973) 7:1470–1472.

Instant Information
How To Locate
Twelve Important Places
in Israel
אֶרֶץ יִשְׂרָאֵל

The source:

סֹבּוּ צִיוֹן וְהַקִּיפוּהָ:

"Walk around Zion, circle it" (Ps. 48:13).

What you need to know:

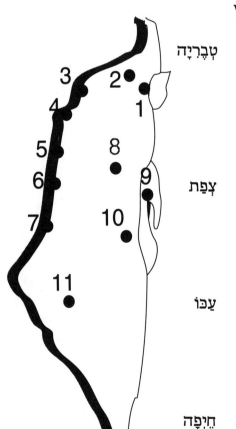

טְבֶרְיָה

1. Tiberias (*Teverya*): A popular holiday resort, it is located in the north on the west shore of the Kinneret (Sea of Galilee). One of the four holy cities of the Jewish people, Tiberias is rich in historical and religious interest. A main attraction is the synagogue, which was built in the third century.

צְפַת

2. Safed (*Tzefat*): Located in the upper Galil (Galilean mountains), twenty-two miles from Tiberias. One of the four holy cities of the Jewish people and the center of the mystics, its attractions today include several old synagogues and the artists colony.

עַכּוּ

3. Acre (*Akko*): From ancient times until the nineteenth century, Acre was the most important seaport in Palestine. Today its attractions include the remainder of a Crusader city. It is located fourteen miles north of Haifa on the Mediterranean Sea.

חֵיפָה

4. Haifa (*Chaifa*): Haifa is Israel's chief port, lying on the northern slopes of Mount Carmel. Its attractions today include the Bahai Shrine and Garden, the Haifa

156

Museum, the Maritime Museum, and the Carmelit (Israel's only subway).

5. Caesarea (*Kaysaria*): This ancient city lies half-way between Tel Aviv and Haifa. Its archaeological ruins include a Roman theater which offers musical concerts in the summer. Its golf course is another popular attraction.   קֵיסָרְיָה

6. Tel Aviv: Located some forty miles northwest of Jerusalem on the Mediterranean Sea, Tel Aviv is the hub of Israel's commerce. Among its many places of interest are the Diaspora Museum, the Great Synagogue, the Israel National Museum, the Carmel Market, the Tel Aviv Museum, and the beaches.   תֵּל אָבִיב

7. Ashkelon: Located thirty-five miles south of Tel Aviv on the Mediterranean Sea, its history goes back to the days of the Canaanites and Philistines. Its archaeological sites are popular tourist attractions along with its extensive bathing beach.   אַשְׁקְלוֹן

8. Jerusalem (*Yerushalayim*): The capital of Israel, Jerusalem is undoubtedly Israel's most historic city. It is one of the four holy cities of Judaism. Among its many sights are the Bezalel Art School, the Biblical Zoo, Hebrew University, the Israel Museum, the Kennedy Memorial, the Knesset (Israel's Parliament), the Western Wall, the Yad VaShem Holocaust Museum, and Hadassah Hospital with its Chagall Windows.   יְרוּשָׁלַיִם

9. Dead Sea (*Yam Hamelech*): This is the lowest place on the earth's surface, forty-seven miles long and ten miles wide. At Ein Gedi, located on the west shore, one can float in the Dead Sea and visit the hot springs.   יָם הַמֶּלַח

10. Masada (*Metzada*): Located on the Dead Sea and rising 1,424 feet above sea level, Masada is most noted as the place where the Zealots managed to hold out against the Romans for three years after the   מְצָדָה

fall of Jerusalem. Its sights include the archaeological remains of the stronghold, including the ancient synagogue where many American tourists celebrate a Bar or Bat Mitzvah.

בְּאֵר שֶׁבַע 11. Beersheba (*Bersheva*): Known as the city of the patriarchs because of its many references in the Five Books of Moses, today Beersheba has become the "capital" of the south. Among its many attractions are the Desert Research Institute and Ben-Gurion University.

אֵילַת 12. Eilat: The southernmost town of Israel, it is situated on the northern end of the Red Sea. It is a popular tourist attraction with its dry hot climate and excellent coral beaches.

Things to remember:

1. One always makes *aliyah* (going up) to Israel and specifically to Jerusalem. When you leave, it is always a *yerida* (going down).

Key words and phrases:

Tel Aviv תֵּל אָבִיב. Literally, mound of spring.
Yam Hamelach יָם הַמֶּלַח. Dead Sea (literally salty sea).

If you want to know more:

David Bamberger, *A Young Person's History of Israel* (New York, 1985).
Encyclopaedia Judaica (Jerusalem, 1975) 9:107 ff.
Zev Vilnay, *Guide to Israel* (Jerusalem, 1978).

Instant Information
Psalm for Pilgrimage
to Jerusalem
עֲלִיָּה לָרֶגֶל

The source:

עָמְדוֹת הָיוּ רַגְלֵינוּ בִּשְׁעָרַיִךְ יְרוּשָׁלָיִם: יְרוּשָׁלַיִם הַבְּנוּיָה כְּעִיר
שֶׁחֻבְּרָה־לָּה יַחְדָּו:

Psalm 122:2–3.

What you need to know:

Our feet are standing at your gates, Jerusalem. Jerusalem, built as a city bound firmly together, where tribes once went up to give thanks unto Adonai, where thrones of justice were once set, thrones of the house of David. Pray for the peace of Jerusalem; may those who love her prosper. May peace be in her walls, tranquility in her towers. May Adonai bless us from Zion and let us see the good of Jerusalem. Let us see our children's children and peace upon Israel.

> Adapted from Psalm 122
> for use at Hebrew Union College
> –Jewish Institute of Religion, Jerusalem

Things to remember:

1. Jews used to make three annual pilgrimages to Jerusalem (for the three major festivals of Sukkot, Pesach, and Shavuot). There they sang the Psalms of Ascent.

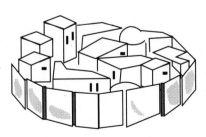

2. When you take a trip to Israel, remember to say this psalm when you arrive in Jerusalem.

3. One always goes up to Jerusalem, physically and spiritually.

Key words and phrases:

Shir hamaalot שִׁיר הַמַּעֲלוֹת. Song of ascending to Jerusalem.

If you want to know more:

Chaya Burstein, *A Kid's Catalogue of Israel* (Philadelphia, 1988).

Barbara Sofer, *Kids Love Israel, Israel Loves Kids* (Rockville, Md., 1981).

Instant Information
Tefillat Haderech
(Prayer said on traveling or taking a trip)
תְּפִלַת הַדֶּרֶךְ

The source:

יְהִי רָצוֹן מִלְּפָנֶיךָ, יְיָ אֱלֹהֵינוּ וֵאלֹהֵי אֲבוֹתֵינוּ, שֶׁתּוֹלִיכֵנוּ
לְשָׁלוֹם וְתַצְעִידֵנוּ לְשָׁלוֹם, וְתַגִּיעֵנוּ אֶל מְחוֹז חֶפְצֵנוּ לְחַיִּים
וּלְשִׂמְחָה וּלְשָׁלוֹם. וְתַצִּילֵנוּ מִכַּף כָּל אוֹיֵב וְאוֹרֵב וְאָסוֹן בַּדֶּרֶךְ,
וְתִתְּנֵנוּ לְחֵן וּלְחֶסֶד וּלְרַחֲמִים בְּעֵינֶיךָ וּבְעֵינֵי כָל רוֹאֵינוּ.
וְתִשְׁמַע קוֹל תַּחֲנוּנֵינוּ, כִּי אֵל שׁוֹמֵעַ תְּפִלָּה וְתַחֲנוּן אָתָּה.
בָּרוּךְ אַתָּה, יְיָ, שׁוֹמֵעַ תְּפִלָּה:

Babylonian Talmud, Berachot 29b.

What you need to know:

May it be Your will, Adonai, my God and God of my ancestors, to lead me, to direct my steps, and to support me along the way. Lead me throughout my life, tranquil and serene, until I arrive at where I am going. Deliver me from every enemy, conflict, and hurt that I might encounter along the way, and from all painful afflictions that trouble the world.

Bless all that I do. Let me receive Your divine grace and mercy. Let me also be the recipient of the loving acts of kindness of all those I meet. Listen to the voice of my appeal, for You are a God who responds to pleas and prayers. Praised are You, Adonai, who hearkens to prayer. Amen.

Things to remember:

1. In some communities, additional scriptural verses are read, as well as Psalms 91 and 121.

Key words and phrases:

Haderech הַדֶּרֶךְ. The road or way.
Nesiah tovah נְסִיעָה טוֹבָה. Have a nice trip (a way of saying goodbye).
Tefillah תְּפִילָה. Prayer.

If you want to know more:

Steven M. Brown, *Higher and Higher* (New York, 1979).

Instant Information
Kaddish Derabbanan
קַדִּישׁ דְּרַבָּנָן

The sources:

1) Babylonian Talmud Sotah 49a.
   2) Seder Eliyahu Rabba, chapter 5.

What you need to know:

יִתְגַּדַּל וְיִתְקַדַּשׁ שְׁמֵהּ רַבָּא. בְּעָלְמָא דִּי בְרָא כִרְעוּתֵהּ וְיַמְלִיךְ מַלְכוּתֵהּ, בְּחַיֵּיכוֹן וּבְיוֹמֵיכוֹן וּבְחַיֵּי דְכָל בֵּית יִשְׂרָאֵל, בַּעֲגָלָא וּבִזְמַן קָרִיב, וְאִמְרוּ אָמֵן:
יְהֵא שְׁמֵהּ רַבָּא מְבָרַךְ לְעָלַם וּלְעָלְמֵי עָלְמַיָּא:
יִתְבָּרַךְ וְיִשְׁתַּבַּח וְיִתְפָּאַר וְיִתְרוֹמַם וְיִתְנַשֵּׂא וְיִתְהַדָּר וְיִתְעַלֶּה וְיִתְהַלָּל שְׁמֵהּ דְּקוּדְשָׁא, בְּרִיךְ הוּא. לְעֵלָּא (בעשי״ת לְעֵלָּא מִכָּל) מִן כָּל בִּרְכָתָא וְשִׁירָתָא, תֻּשְׁבְּחָתָא וְנֶחֱמָתָא, דַּאֲמִירָן בְּעָלְמָא, וְאִמְרוּ אָמֵן:
עַל יִשְׂרָאֵל וְעַל רַבָּנָן וְעַל תַּלְמִידֵיהוֹן וְעַל כָּל תַּלְמִידֵי תַלְמִידֵיהוֹן, וְעַל כָּל מָאן דְּעָסְקִין בְּאוֹרַיְתָא, דִּי בְּאַתְרָא הָדֵין וְדִי בְכָל אֲתַר וַאֲתַר, יְהֵא לְהוֹן וּלְכוֹן שְׁלָמָא רַבָּא חִנָּא וְחִסְדָּא וְרַחֲמִין וְחַיִּין אֲרִיכִין וּמְזוֹנָא רְוִיחֵי וּפוּרְקָנָא מִן קֳדָם אֲבוּהוֹן דְּבִשְׁמַיָּא וְאַרְעָא וְאִמְרוּ אָמֵן:
יְהֵא שְׁלָמָא רַבָּא מִן שְׁמַיָּא וְחַיִּים טוֹבִים עָלֵינוּ וְעַל כָּל יִשְׂרָאֵל וְאִמְרוּ אָמֵן:
עוֹשֶׂה שָׁלוֹם בִּמְרוֹמָיו הוּא בְּרַחֲמָיו יַעֲשֶׂה שָׁלוֹם עָלֵינוּ וְעַל כָּל יִשְׂרָאֵל וְאִמְרוּ אָמֵן:

Yitgadal v'yitkadash sh'mei raba b'alma di v'ra chir'utei,
v'yamlich malchutei b'chayeichon u-v'yomeichon u-vchayei
d'chol beit yisrael, ba-agala u-vi-z'man kariv, v'imru amen.
Y'hei sh'mei raba m'varach l'alam u'l'almei almaya.
Yitbarach v'yishtabach v'yitpa'ar v'yitromam v'yitnasei,
v'yit'hadar v'yit'aleh v'yit-halal sh'mei d'kudsha, b'rich hu
l'eila (l'eila mi-kol) min kol birchata v'shirata, tushbechata
v'nechemata da-amiran b'alma, v'imru amen.
Al yisrael v'al rabbanan v'al talmideihon, v'al kol talmidei

*talmideihon, v'al kol man d'askin b'oraita, di v'atra ha-
dein v'di b'chol atar v'atar, y'hei l'hon u-l'chon sh'lama
raba, china v'chisda v'rachamin, v'chayin arichin u-
mzona r'vichei, u-furkana min kodam avuhon di vi-
sh'maya v'ar'a, v'imru amen.
Y'hei sh'lama raba min sh'maya ve'chayim tovim aleinu
v'al kol yisrael, v'imru amen.
Oseh shalom bi-m'romav, hu b'rachamav ya'aseh shalom
aleinu v'al kol yisrael, v'imru amen.*

Exalted and hallowed be God's great name. In this
world of Your creation. May Your will be fulfilled and
Your Sovereignty revealed. In the days of your lifetime
and the life of the whole house of Israel speedily and
soon, and say, Amen.

Be Your great name blessed forever, indeed, to all
eternity.

Be the name of the most Holy Blessed One praised
and honored, extolled and glorified, adored and exalted supremely. Beyond all blessings and hymns,
praises and consolations that may be uttered in this
world, and say, Amen.

May we of Israel and our rabbis, their disciples, and
all their pupils, and all who engage in the study
of Torah here and everywhere, find abundant peace,
gracious favor and mercy, long life, ample sustenance
and liberation through their Parent in heaven, and
say, Amen.

May peace abundant descend from Heaven with a
good life for us and for all Israel, and say, Amen.

May You Who creates the harmony of the spheres
create peace in Your tender love for us and for all
Israel, and say, Amen.

Things to remember:

1. *Kaddish Derabbanan* is said after public study of sacred
   literature.

2. Often a small section of Mishna is read at the conclusion of a regular service in order to provide people
   with an opportunity to recite this *Kaddish.*

3. Since the Holocaust, it is a practice in some synagogues to routinely recite this *Kaddish* in memory of all of the martyred teachers who perished.

4. *Kaddish Derabbanan,* like the other *Kaddish* prayers, is written in Aramaic (a sister language to Hebrew).

5. *Kaddish* prayers are used both to affirm belief in God and to separate different sections of the liturgy. (They function like special commas and periods.)

6. *Kaddish Derabbanan* is said while standing.

7. Out of respect for our teachers, it is a custom to actually read the words each time you say *Kaddish* even if you know the prayer by memory.

Key words and phrases

Kaddish derabbanan קַדִּישׁ דְּרַבָּנָן (Aramaic). Literally, the Rabbis' *Kaddish.*

If you want to know more:

Steven M. Brown, *Higher and Higher* (New York, 1979).